Linda:

Be you to fullness

Russell Scott

AWAKENING THE GURU IN YOU

ENLIGHTENMENT THROUGH CONSCIOUS COMMUNICATION

– THE CO-EVOLUTION PROCESS –

RUSSELL SCOTT

BALBOA.
PRESS
A DIVISION OF HAY HOUSE

Balboa Press books may be ordered through booksellers or by contacting:

Balboa Press
A Division of Hay House
1663 Liberty Drive
Bloomington, IN 47403
www.balboapress.com
1-(877) 407-4847

Because of the dynamic nature of the Internet, any web addresses or links contained in
this book may have changed since publication and may no longer be valid. The views
expressed in this work are solely those of the author and do not necessarily reflect the
views of the publisher, and the publisher hereby disclaims any responsibility for them.

The author of this book does not dispense medical advice or prescribe the use
of any technique as a form of treatment for physical, emotional, or medical
problems without the advice of a physician, either directly or indirectly. The
intent of the author is only to offer information of a general nature to help you
in your quest for emotional and spiritual well-being. In the event you use any
of the information in this book for yourself, which is your constitutional right,
the author and the publisher assume no responsibility for your actions.

Any people depicted in stock imagery provided by Thinkstock are models,
and such images are being used for illustrative purposes only.
Certain stock imagery © Thinkstock.

Printed in the United States of America.

ISBN: 978-1-4525-7853-8 (sc)
ISBN: 978-1-4525-7855-2 (hc)
ISBN: 978-1-4525-7854-5 (e)

Library of Congress Control Number: 2013913261

Balboa Press rev. date: 09/06/2013

DOGMA-FREE ZONE

I think we should all have a dogma-free zone
Somewhere in our world.
A place:
Where we can think our own thoughts and listen to own our voice.
Where all beliefs are considered as assumptions until we can directly
experience them for ourselves
Where the "truth" is not considered a four-letter word.
A guru-free zone:
Where we can bow down to ourselves and honour our own wisdom
Where Buddhists can grow their hair really long and
All Christians, Hindus, Jews, and Sikhs can hang-up their sacred hats
before they enter
(and when they leave, will put on someone else's hat)
A place where fundamentalists, if they enter, will explode from their
own inner bombast.
A spiritual name-free zone
Where we can pretend we are Popeye and say
"I yam what I yam" and totally accept ourselves.
Where we can look in the mirror without fear and see total
magnificence
A place where, when everything seems to be falling apart,
we can let go
and let it fall into place
Where we can be okay about not knowing anything
and allow ourselves to experience everything . . .
exactly the way it is.
That would be a great place.
I think we all should start by writing "Dogma-free zone" on a sticker
Slap it on our forehead and look at each other . . .
Then laugh our heads off!

Russell Scott, July 2008

CONTENTS

INTRODUCTION

The Fallen Hierarchy

For over twenty-five years, I have been working with individuals to help them discover their real purpose in life, to awaken to the magnificence of their true nature and to assist them in dissolving the reactive mind. This allowed them to begin to create their lives from the truth of themselves, instead of re-manifesting the same old suffering.

In 2009, I burnt out. I reached a point where I had been pushing the river too much, so to speak, in giving too many one-to-one sessions and workshops. Although I had not recognized the degree of my burnout, a good friend of mine did and she invited me down to her villa in Belize to stay with her and her husband for a week to recuperate. I had been feeling a growing sense of discouragement in how the world seemed to counteract genuine spiritual development and how, in many ways, it labeled spiritual seekers as heady impractical weirdoes with nothing of substance to contribute to the ambient consumer culture.

I was seriously thinking of giving up the task of helping others awaken. I was feeling like my time was up as a personal transformation facilitator and was planning on going out and getting a "Joe" job where I could experience the no-thinking mind state of working in a multi-national chain store, taking merchandise out of boxes and putting it on shelves. Perhaps I had missed the point of life, and restocking store shelves was really nirvana. Or maybe what I was really looking for was something to re-inspire me.

So I went to Belize. I spent a lot of time sleeping and enjoying the sun and heat in a welcomed respite from the Canadian winter. I thought that my trip was really all about resting. But on my fourth day I thought about going back home and wondered what I'd say to people about what I did while I was in Belize. I decided that I'd do something touristy. At least I could say I did something other than sleep in the hot sun. I decided to visit a pyramid site thinking that the visit would fit into the category of the mystical and would satisfy some of my spiritual friends.

I booked a trip to Lamanai, one of the oldest pyramid sites in Central America. It took us about an hour to boat up the river as it was in a secluded part of the country in an unpopulated area off the eastern coast of Belize.

We toured a number of the smaller pyramids on the site. When I got to the largest pyramid I was inspired to climb to the top of the pyramid to take in a brief meditation. A number of other tourists had also made the climb to the top and for a while there was a crowd of people looking around, gabbing and enjoying the view. I thought that there was no way I would get some time to myself but then suddenly everyone left and I was left at the top alone. I managed to stand there with my eyes closed, in silence, for about three minutes before the tour guide yelled from the bottom for me to come down.

But that was enough . . . I felt a vague sense of something shift in me but I didn't know what it was at the time. When I came down from the pyramid I found myself walking beside the tour guide and decided to take advantage of the coincidence by asking him about his personal interest in the Mayans. It turned out that he had a degree in archaeology and was an expert on Mayan culture.

I asked him about his theory on why the Mayan civilization disappeared (having read different explanations in a number of publications over the last year including the popular new-age explanation that the culture had "ascended").

The guide began with his summary. He told me that the decline of the culture was the result of two things: the ego aggrandizement of the Emperors and the hierarchical system of religion and governance. He explained that the pyramids were built as monuments to each Emperor. As each new Emperor installed himself, he had to build over the face and top of each pyramid built by his predecessor to emphasize his prominence. To do this, the Mayans needed more lime to cement the stones in place. In order to get the lime cement, they had to burn the limestone in the area with wood from the trees that were growing in the vicinity. As more and more trees were cut and burned and the landscape denuded, the climate got drier and hotter. Without the moderating effect of the trees on the wind and temperature, the crops failed.

He further related that Mayan culture was based on a multi-god religion and power was vested exclusively by the priests and kings. The rulers became more and more removed from their underlings and gradually lost touch with the actual conditions of daily life as experienced by the people. Instead of realizing the consequences of their egotistical actions on the environment, they thought that the solution was to appease the gods with human sacrifices. The High Priests put fear into the minds of the people with threats that if the gods were not pleased, there would be disaster.

For many years, the populace accepted this practice. It was part of their religion. It was part of their culture. They were raised from birth to death under the doctrine that was passed on down the line from the Emperor, to the High Priest, to the Initiates and to them. They were indoctrinated. What else could they do but believe in the divine decree of the Emperor? But of course the sacrifices never worked, there were more and more crop failures and people began starving.

As food resources dwindled, city-states that were once in peaceful co-existence began to invade one another convincing the people that the other city-states were enemies. The conquerors robbed the conquered of food and riches and subjected those they vanquished to slavery. After decades of environmental devastation, food shortages, sacrifices and war, many of the populace got fed up with the sacrificing of their husbands, wives and children and those who didn't starve eventually walked into the jungle. (One might say that the Emperors then "ass-ended").

After the guide finished his summary, he looked at me and continued walking. His silence spoke volumes: "Same old history, brand-new news."

I was shocked at how history was repeating itself. And although I was not sure of the veracity of the tour guide's historical summary, I saw the connection. We have environmental degradation caused by over-consumption of resources, de-forestation, and the political elite that dictates to the masses and manipulates them to fear their neighbors. We have sacrificed our children to the gods of war in the name of creating peace. We have invaded other countries to secure their resources. We have various religious authorities that have programmed their followers to believe that the way to heaven is to subjugate those who do not follow their same path.

Although I was aware of this before, it became even clearer to me how easily the political and religious elite can manipulate a population to believe whatever they want them to believe. There are many examples in our own time of how a mass culture can become a mass cult, galvanized around a few charismatic leaders whose oratorical and personal powers are sufficiently advanced to alter people's perceptions of reality, even to the point where people will put their own lives in jeopardy to support a lie. How did we come to believe that there were weapons of mass destruction in Iraq? Did we really believe that Jews are an inferior race and must be eliminated?

And in the religious sphere, history is replete with examples of self-appointed spiritual leaders, promising nirvana and a blissful afterlife and then leading followers down a path of mind control, financial poverty, physical abuse, sexual predatorship and even suicide. One does not need to search very far to find examples: the death cult of Reverend Jim Jones, the sexual and child abuse inherent in the polygamous offshoots of the Mormon Church, the multimillion dollar lawsuits being faced by the Catholic Church.

I have always known that behind the pain and suffering of followers seduced by charismatic leaders and teachers, truth is the sacrificial victim of political and religious dogma. But when the tour guide looked at me after relaying his story, it was as if I suddenly realized the extent to which this pattern reaches back far into our human history and is still carrying on in our consciousness.

Why? The question stopped me in my tracks.

I thought about the years and years I'd spent searching for the truth, employing various techniques to help people reach spiritual realization for themselves. I thought about the 11 years I'd spent running a retreat centre witnessing and participating in events that helped people come to inner peace and connect to their true selves. I'd thought also about how I'd been seduced into a cult many years ago and experienced the damage to others and myself. I mentally sorted through the filing card box full of memories searching for the answer.

Then, for some reason, I looked back at that huge Mayan pyramid. When I took in its imposing presence on the landscape and in its enormity, the reason suddenly became clear. It was the way that the deception was delivered. The problem was the pyramidal structure, the hierarchy: Emperor to Priest to Initiate to Populace; Pope to Bishop to Priest to Congregation; Guru to Chela; Teacher to Student, Author to Reader. The idea that one's personal evolution is totally dependent on receiving the truth from another, who is supposedly more enlightened, more advanced, more exalted and more knowledgeable—that was the problem. Yes, there were other factors involved but the fundamental problem was the structure— the hierarchical structure.

When there is a socialized perception that those higher up the political and religious ladder are more spiritually-evolved, automatically we tend to believe that truth and knowledge is more accessible to the ones higher up rather than to ourselves. We believe that truth is acquired from without rather than inspired from within and that it is dependent on a teacher's exposition rather than our own exploration. Within the hierarchical structure, people are likely to accept dogma as truth rather than depending on their own discrimination.

At this point, with this new insight in mind, I re-joined the group of tourists and the realization retreated into the back of my mind. I completed the tour of Lamanai and returned back to my room. As I drifted off to sleep, I re-lived the whole scene and began to ponder the question. "Well if the hierarchical approach is problematic to spiritual growth, what is the better way?"

The next morning I awoke with the mental image of that huge pyramid rising out of the jungle. The question persisted: "How does consciousness evolve in the most optimal way?" As I sat with the question, my mind was drawn to a vision of the jungle itself, the environment out of which the pyramid had arisen, and the penny dropped. It was simple. I saw it in the nature of the forest itself. I saw each element in the forest: the trees, the insects, the animals, the plants in the under story, the soil organisms all evolving together. "Life evolves in relationship".

It was clear that consciousness did not evolve as the result of one person delivering his idea of truth down the line so that those below accepted it as second-hand belief. It evolved in a more democratic process of equals relating to one another and it was far more effective. Just as many organisms in the forest adapted and evolved symbiotically to their present state, so too in our interactions and relating to one another that we evolve. We evolve together in a very organic, democratic process. The name came to me: "Co-evolution".

As I sat with this new piece of the puzzle fitting together, a final piece clicked in: "Russell, you are already leading people through this process."

For the last twenty-five years, I had been leading people through many seminars and retreats using a process where people sat in dyads (two people) or small groups, where they inquired into personal and ultimate questions of life and shared their thoughts and experiences. As people related with each other, they arrived at deep personal insights, let go of internal blocks and awakened to the divine nature of their existence. I did not teach any dogma or philosophy. I only taught a contemplation and communication technique and people naturally evolved as the result of practicing it. I never had a label or fitting term to explain what it was that I did. But this new term "Co-evolution" wrapped up what I was doing into a neat little bundle. I found that this new label carried a lot of power; it could easily be understood and it communicated the immense benefits people were receiving from the method. With this came the inspiration to share this concept through a book to a wider audience. And this, with a lot of excitement, is what I am doing now.

WHY I WROTE THIS BOOK

I must honestly say that before my trip to Belize, I never intended to write this book. It was never in the vision of my life to be an author. Nor was it ever in my plans to become a spiritual teacher. (I have checked in my high school yearbook and "the person most likely to be a guru" was never there). Some people are motivated to do these things out of a desire for fame, adulation and riches or power. Other people consciously do these things altruistically out of a sincere desire to help people find inner peace and contribute to a better world. This was never the case for me. I was always an undemonstrative seeker of truth. When that naturally evolved into a desire to share the techniques that helped me awaken and then realized that this meant I was to become a spiritual teacher, I ran kicking and screaming the other way.

In a similar way, I have become a reluctant author. I am still dumbfounded that this book got completed. I would have much preferred to just lay on the couch watching hockey than have spiritual aspirants and teachers get annoyed at me for pointing out their dogmatic wiles. But the book kept poking at me like a dog begging for treats. It kept staring at me, no matter how many ways I tried to avoid its gaze, I eventually succumbed to its begging.

If I was able to give the best explanation, I'd say that the book was roaming around somewhere in the ethers desperately looking for someone to give birth to it. It saw some unwitting fellow have a powerful experience on top of a pyramid and then latched onto him as he opened up. So when the original idea of the book came to me, I thought it would be just a presentation of the Co-evolution Process, but as it emerged I recognized that it needed to become something else, something more than I had planned: a manifesto for the spiritual anarchist, a questioning of those in a position of spiritual authority, a challenge to truth seekers to respond to this hierarchy with self-reliance, accountability and responsibility and a delineation of the genuine path to enlightenment so that seekers can be freed of limited or even delusory spiritual experiences.

In short, it had another purpose: to release us from the prison of religious indoctrination and to offer a superior alternative to the "dogma guru", i.e. the real guru within.

So just like a young mother, I have struggled through all the resistances and joys of pregnancy and finally given birth and now recognize the beauty and blessing of what has come . . . a bringing forth from the old ways, a new method of opening up into the mystery of Self and seeing into the nature of existence.

There is one proviso in all of this that needs to be made clear. I am aware that I am walking a thin path of paradox. In offering up my wisdom to you about truth, the spiritual path to awakening and dogma gurus, I could very well be creating in you another set of beliefs or dogma that can imprison you. To prevent this, I ask you to not believe anything I present to you and also not to disbelieve what I write. I ask you to consider it and dwell somewhere in the zone between openness and skepticism, the unknown and the certain, and to treat this as a hypothesis until you, yourself, in your own experience, discover it to be true or not. I ask you to try out the co-evolution exercises at the back of the book with some fellow spiritual cohorts and see what you think.

My greatest wish is that you get turned on like me and thousands of others to the liberating power of the Co-Evolution process so that you too use it to transform your life and become your own guru. Your experience will be the proof in the pudding . . . then the final word is yours.

WHO THIS BOOK IS FOR

On the outside we look like everybody else. We talk, walk, eat, sleep, work, relax, earn money, pay bills, wake, dream . . . but on the inside we feel different. We question, we search . . . we are yearning . . . for a meaning and a truth deeper than what our culture has offered us. We were taught it's on the outside but we have been disappointed to find out it's not. So we are searching for a way of being and relating that comes from who we really are that is genuine, real and compassionate, looking for a purpose to our lives that gives everything a deeper meaning and for a way to connect to others and the world so that we feel we belong to the mystery that is grander than ourselves. And sometimes we feel alone on the path because we are not willing to settle for someone else's truth. But that is the price we are willing to pay for wanting to live from the place that we now know is the only place to live . . . from the inside out.

Some of us are Boomers. We made it through most of our lives and there is still a remnant of the hippie inside. We look back at the picture of when we were children and wondered what happened to us? Where did that shining presence go? What's it all about? Who did I become? There is a vague sense of emptiness and a yearning inside but the yearning somehow feels natural . . . something that will eventually lead us to a deeper experience of life.

Some of us are on the other end of life. We are young and in our twenties just entering the world. We feel a lot of apprehension in merging with the consumer culture. We want to treat each other well.

We want to treat the world right. We wonder if there is something deeper than the shallow life that we judge most everyone lives on the outside. There is a vague sense of emptiness and a yearning inside but the yearning somehow feels natural . . . something that will eventually lead us to a deeper experience of life.

Some of us are stuck in the middle. We work and maybe have a family. We feel trapped in the routine, the responsibilities and the necessities of life. The world just seems too big for us to change. Even though it's hard for us to take time for ourselves, we know that it is the inside that needs to change first. That's where it all begins. There is a vague sense of emptiness and a yearning inside but the yearning somehow feels natural . . . something that will eventually lead us to a greater deeper of life.

Some of us are hurt. It doesn't matter how old we are, we've been banged up by life pretty bad. We've tried a lot of things in order to feel better that have turned out to be not so good. We've read the self-help books, listened to the CD's. They are piled up beside the bed . . . lots of ideas. We've looked for relief and now we want something deeper. We want resolution. We are looking for our true heart in a world that's fallen apart. There is a vague sense of emptiness and a yearning inside but the yearning somehow feels natural . . . something that will eventually lead us to a deeper experience of life.

Some of us just are inherently spiritual. We were born that way. It's always been with us. We naturally investigate. We throw ourselves into life. We are in touch with the deeper essence of ourselves and want to expand and shine. We have a hard time being materialistic because we know the juice is somewhere else. We are suspicious of authorities, even spiritual authorities, because we know the ultimate truth is in ourselves. There is a vague sense of emptiness and a yearning inside but the yearning somehow feels natural . . . something that will eventually lead us to a deeper experience of life.

We are the ones I call the *Mystic Misfits*. We aren't interested in dogma. We realize that a good portion of our culture is indoctrinated. It's a "cult"-ure. It's just more of the same old same old. We only take what confirms and expands what we have already experienced and let go of the rest. The idea of a dogmatic guru gives us a rash. We've tried to have someone else save us and it hasn't worked.

We don't fit the guru/dogma mould. The only place we are ever going to fit is into our true selves. We prefer to stare into the unknown forever until the teacher within shows up, rather than sit on a cushion and be spoon-fed someone else's version of reality. We are here to discover the truth of ourselves for ourselves, genuinely connect to others and offer our uniqueness to the world. And the good news is this . . . it's not necessary for us to be the lone ranger. Yes, we have to do it by ourselves but we don't have to do it alone anymore. There's too many of us now. We can do it alone, together.

For now let's call this Co-evolution. That's what I am calling it. You can call it whatever you want later. After reading what I have to say, you can call me nuts or inspired. That's your prerogative as a *Mystic Misfit* because you don't need a license to evaluate what's true or not, call things the way they are or even be yourself.

Let us follow that deep yearning for the truth to find the real teacher within and our true spiritual path, the journey of evolving together in our ordinary lives.

We are the ones we have been waiting for.

The saviour is us!

So with long introductions completed, we can begin with one of the things that has started our seeking for the inner guru: our skepticism of the outer guru. Let us chomp into the 'meat of the matter'.

CHAPTER 1

HOLY COW HAMBURGER

The guru tradition has been an ancient tradition in the east for centuries. Spiritual teachers have been a respected part of spiritual practice and their wisdom and guidance has been honoured as an essential aspect of everyday life. Within the Eastern religions, there are elaborate codes of conduct which both preserve the stability of life within the religious order and set them apart from the popular culture. These traditions emphasize the sublimation of personal will and ego identification in favour of worship, service and conformity to spiritual authority.

But as spiritual teachers have migrated to the West, a place that emphasizes individuality, laissez-fare morality and capitalism, the results have been confusing and sometimes painful. Our culture has turned these eastern holy-cows into hamburgers.

The West has also produced its own, home-grown, self-appointed teachers, anointed by their own professed divine revelations. They have seduced many of their followers with their charisma and personal power. They have told us their version of reality is the one to believe. Many individuals have been seriously misled through abuses of sex, money and power and even encouraged to commit serious crimes or suicide on behalf of these self-anointed gurus. The practices, beliefs and rituals of these men and women have quite rightly been met with derision, leaving many serious spiritual seekers quite harmed, wary and angry at the whole scene.

In addition, we have seen a merging and blending of many traditions leading to new creative iterations of practices and beliefs: yoga and aerobics, shamanism and energy therapy, Buddhism and psychotherapy. I've even come across a practice that combined native spirituality, kabbalah study and rebounding called "Yahoo-ism". The variety of these combinations and the hype around their effectiveness is dizzying. When established traditions are combined with new untested practices and then re-branded with creative marketing, the spiritual consumer has a hard time deciding the efficacy and authenticity of these teachers, their beliefs and practices. Some of these new combinations are untested and dangerous while others have produced some remarkable improvements over age-old traditions.

We are also experiencing a blending of spirituality and capitalism delivered in over-priced, under-delivered seminars that somehow equates financial abundance with higher consciousness, and self-worth with net worth. These movements prey on people's fears and dreams of easy riches, promoting greed, while sinking their students deeper into a you-can-have-it-all materialism and, all too often, debt. Self-help books offer a pre-packaged set of beliefs and quick fixes that leave people feeling a sense of self-helplessness, failure and cynicism rather than deep transformation.

I have personally had both positive and negative experiences with teachers over the years. I have experienced the emotional pain of being part of a dogmatic spiritual cult and another psychotherapeutic cult with my marriage damaged and good friends estranged. I have witnessed the harm that resulted when sociopathic gurus were caught with their pants down, their hands in the till or their golden shoes fastened to the pedestal. Many gurus have used brilliant transformation methods to scam others for their own selfish means. They have led people to discredit genuine advanced spiritual practices and have thrown the baby out with the bathwater. I have also counseled seekers who have been mentally and psychologically injured because they blindly placed their trust in the dogma and unhealthy practices of their mentors.

Yet on the other hand, I have experienced immense benefits, including powerful divine awakening experiences, gained under the mentorship of several spiritual guides. These people have supported me with love and firmness. They have helped me through barriers on the path that I could not have overcome on my own. As well, in my 11-year tenure as the owner of the Ecology Retreat Centre in Ontario, Canada, I have had the pleasure, and sometimes disappointment, of interacting with many spiritual teachers, gurus, seminar leaders and personal growth facilitators. As a result, I have been exposed to a wide spectrum of wisdom teachers and spiritual paths, some who are genuine and life affirming, and some who are harmful, misguided and downright weird.

It is no wonder that the whole spiritual scene has come under scrutiny. People are wondering if there is any value in having a guru and following any form of tradition.

Yes, the West has made hamburger out of the "Holy Cows" in the guru tradition and although it has been disheartening for some, others like me have seen the blessing behind the curse. For too long we have looked on dogma as the necessary evil that comes with the guru in order for us to advance on the spiritual path. *Now we are seeing clearly that dogma is the* unnecessary veil *between the divine and ourselves* and we no longer want it. Let it be understood that I am not advising anyone not to follow a guru or to just follow your own intuition blindly without external guidance. These choices must be personal options, but we must not make them blindly. There is much to consider even before we make these decisions.

CHAPTER 2

THE FIRST QUESTIONS

DO I NEED A GURU?

"For everyone there is a guru. I admit a guru for myself, too. Who is my guru? . . . The guru is the Self,"

—Ramana Maharshi

"Do I need a guru?

"What do I gain from having one?"

"Can I get enlightened without one?"

"If I do require one, what kind of guru do I need?"

"How can I avoid dogma?"

"How can I recognize what a true teacher is?"

"What are the conditions for me to become my own guru?"

These are all very crucial considerations for anyone on a spiritual path. To guru or not to guru . . . that is the question.

But before attempting to answer these questions however, I propose that there are other questions that we need to answer first. These will form a basic understanding from which answers to the

4

above questions can be developed. These are the foundation questions I suggest we consider:

"What is the purpose of a spiritual path?" and

"What is a spiritual path?"

It stands to reason that if we know the purpose of the spiritual path, then we will be able to determine what kind of teacher we need to accomplish that goal. We will be clearer about the path to follow to find the guru inside ourselves. If the aim is to be happy, then maybe we just need a person to tell us jokes all the time. If the aim is to be financially stable, then maybe we need a business coach. If the aim is to have more knowledge, then maybe we require someone to stand at the front of the room and give us lectures. Let us begin our investigation.

WHAT IS THE PURPOSE OF A SPIRITUAL PATH?

Is it to find greater wisdom, make more money, become more successful and accomplished, become calmer, more energetic, feel more fulfilled in life, gain personal mastery or something else? Ask anyone who has a spiritual bent and you will get hundreds of different answers. And believe me I have asked a lot of people. When I ran the Ecology Retreat Centre in Orangeville, Ontario, I asked a lot of people who came there for personal development this question and I got a wide variety of answers. I also did my own research, in the course of delivering my own seminars, by asking people: "what is your highest goal in life?" From both of these sources, the answer seemed to boil down to the similar things. People want to: "be all I can be", "live from the depth of my soul" and "live a life that fully expresses myself". They want to be themselves, fully.

So it seems that people feel that the purpose of a spiritual path is to discover the truth of life, the Self and the Self in relationship to others and to fully manifest that truth. To distill this even further it is simply, people want to "be-you-to-fullness", or live a "Be-You-to-Full" life. We could also call this True-Self-Actualization . . . the full presentation of your true Self in life. It appears that this full engagement of our selves in any activity of life is what brings fulfillment. When we are fully participating in our work, the potential of success is much greater. When we are fully present in our relationships, there is a deeper connection with our partners and more love exchanged. When we are fully present in our recreational activities, we are happier.

You might want to verify this for yourself right now. Go ahead, stop reading for a few moments and feel the rightness or wrongness of these for yourself. Do these statements resonate with you? How do they feel?

Don't read on. Take a minute.

Now that you've considered . . . think of this:. What is it that you are trying to do in leading a spiritual life? Certainly it is something to do with living, right? It's certainly not about dying. It has something to do with being alive. If that is the case then maybe it's about living a better life than the one you have, maybe a happier life—to live in such a way that life is more satisfying, more inspiring? Maybe it's about discovering something deeper about life that can do this for us. Perhaps there is a non-physical realm that can uplift us and inform us. Or maybe the material realm is all there is.

How are we to know what is what?

Well it seems obvious that if we are to find out the answers, we must search for them. We must seek to discover. If this is so, then what are we to discover? I suggest to you that we must discover the truth, because if we just discover something false and try to live from that, we are going to be in trouble. If we believe that there is no food in the house and the truth is that there is a feast in the next room, then we are in danger of starving. If men and women believe that opposite sexes are enemies, then we will never reproduce and the human race is doomed. So we cannot live from falsity. It does not produce a better life.

We need to live from truth.

If upliftment is something we want, then we need to understand what life, others and Self are really all about so that we can at least live in harmony with that reality. If the fulfillment in life comes from our engagement in it, then we need to know what we are engaging in. If we erroneously believe rivers flow up stream and cast our boat downstream from our destination hoping to get there easily by going upstream, we have got a big problem. If we want to be more fulfilled as a person, it also makes sense to know the truth of who we really are and be that. If we believe that we are dogs and some others are cats and start acting as a dog around others who think they are cats, we are also in big trouble. So we need to live in alignment with who we really are, what others are and what life is.

Therefore **the first step on the spiritual path is to know the truth.** Once we know who we really are, what others are and what life is, then there is a great possibility that on a basic level we can live in harmony with these actualities.

So this begs two questions:

1) What is Truth?
2) How do we find the truth?

CHAPTER 3

WHAT IS TRUTH?

As we begin to investigate this question, all kinds of barriers arise that can get in the way. We can feel an aversion to the truth. We can look at the term as one of those profane "four-letter" words even though it is five. The word itself can become associated in our minds with all the so-called truth purveyors who have deceived people with a version of reality that was, in the end, a pack of lies. Millions of people have been killed and hurt in the name of truth. We can get cynical and suspicious of this investigation. We can get entangled and lost in a maze of philosophical investigations about the nature of truth and never find our way out for years. We could decide that truth just can't be known and give up.

It's really not necessary to engage in any of this. Really. There's a simple definition. Over the years and years of being a fanatic at truth-seeking, I have embarrassingly missed the obviousness of its definition.

Are you ready for the shock of its utter simplicity? Are you ready to smack your head and say "Duh?"

The Truth is the way reality actually is.

Let us explore this more deeply.

The truth is not the way we want things to be, the way others view life, the way we feel about something subjectively, the way we define things through our concepts or beliefs, the way we want, affirm or imagine things to be . . . none of this. The truth is the actuality of life, Self and others. It is the fact of something, its essence.

There is the way we think, believe, feel, affirm, perceive or hope things are and then there is the way things—meaning the realities of Self, life and others—actually are. Ultimately any thoughts we come up with about these realities of self, life or others are just that—ideas. Ideas are conceptualizations and, as such, are just pictures in the mind; they are not the real things. When we think of the word "tree" we will access this idea by picturing a tree in our minds. The word itself is not the actual tree; even the reproduction in ours minds is not the real tree.

We can even imagine this tree in our minds and sense or feel ourselves sitting against the tree. The mind is so powerful that we can manufacture an experience that doesn't exist. We can read a book about cosmic consciousness, understand the concept and then imagine ourselves as one with the cosmos, floating everywhere, as a drop in the cosmic ocean and we will definitely feel this. But is it real? No. It is mentally and emotionally constructed.

Truth is in the realm of existence. It is real. It is not made up. It has an actuality and authenticity to it. The truth about something is the core of its verity. When we realize what is not true about ourselves, the falseness vanishes. The untruth disappears. On the other hand when we realize the truth of ourselves, the reality comes more into being or more into conscious awareness.

Truth is also truth because there is a consistency about it. Something that is true continues to be the way it is. There is unchangeableness about it. When we say that something is true, like a true course, we mean that it does not alter. It continues on its path to the goal and does not veer off. There is inevitability about it. It will always be there for us or for another. It is forever. It will not disappear. It will not fade. It continues to be itself no matter what we think about it.

We will expand on the understanding of the nature of truth later in the section on "Direct Experience". But first I invite you to do the following exercise in order to get an idea of what I am talking about. Do this exercise with a chair and sit on it.

THE CHAIR EXERCISE

First, notice what it is that you are sitting on. Be in the feeling of it. Take a few moments to settle into the experience of the chair.

Now get the idea that a special friend spent many hours of labour making the chair for you. They made this out of great connection and friendship for you. They spent hours and hours of loving work to make this for you. Really get into the belief. For a few minutes, imagine this and let it in . . . then note how you feel about the chair.

Shake it off and let that feeling go.

Now get the idea that the colour of the chair is a very unhealthy colour and that science has verified that this particular colour emits toxic carcinogenic radiation that seeps into your skin. Get the idea that a lot of research has been done on this and the toxicity of this colour is a well-established fact. Really get into the belief. For a few minutes imagine this and let it in . . . then note how you feel about the chair.

Shake that off and let that go.

Now get the idea that a very holy person, a spiritually-advanced person whom you greatly admire, spent years and years meditating in this chair. They had many great spiritual realizations while sitting there. Really get into that belief. For a few minutes imagine this and let it in . . . then note how you feel about the chair.

Shake that off and let that feeling go.

Then look at the chair again. Has it changed?

Is it different from the time when you started the exercise?

I'll bet that it is still the same chair as before the exercise.

Well what changed during the exercise?

It was our belief or the way we thought things were. This changed our experience, right? The chair was still a chair all through the exercise. To an outside observer it continued to be the same chair, no matter what you thought.

So the chair is like the Truth: the way reality actually is . . . the way things actually are.

There was the fact of the chair just being a chair and then there was our perception of it. Our experience of the chair was different from the chair itself. It was imposed on the chair. It depended on what we were thinking, not on the actuality of the chair. When we had a different view or belief about the chair, our experience of the chair changed even though the chair stayed the same. It was our thoughts about the chair that changed our experience of the chair, but in reality the actual chair continued to be the same chair even though we had different thoughts about it.

Just like the chair, truth is independent of our thinking. It is not defined by our beliefs. It is separate from our concepts. It is not the label or the name we attach to things. The idea of a mountain is not the mountain. The name of anything is only the label that points to it.

We do not make the mistake of going into a restaurant and eating the menu thinking it is the food. The menu is just a description. Even our understanding and knowledge of a thing is still not the actual thing. We may extensively understand the chemical composition of a peach, be able the identify all of its nutrients and even comprehend the minute interaction that goes on between the juices of the fruit and our taste buds but this is still not the same as actually tasting the peach. Similarly, having an intellectual knowledge of love is not the same as the wonderfully exhilarating feeling of being in love. Therefore, the only experience the mind has is of the thought of a thing, not the thing itself. Its only experience is theoretical not reality.

Yet so often on the spiritual path we think that understanding intellectually the concept of enlightenment, awakening or spirituality is the actual thing. We listen to the guru explaining their understanding of existence and the ideas all make sense, but the beliefs are all second-hand and we take them in as "truth".

We would be repulsed by the idea of swallowing someone else's pre-digested meal yet so often we swallow a guru's predigested belief system whole-heartedly without a gag, a burp or a belch. Certain animals feed their young this way and this is how they mature, but eventually they grow up and go out and seek their own nurturance. If we are to become self-sufficient in our spiritual development, surely we should move beyond this stage of spoon-fed infancy, beyond the deception that thought, concepts, names, ideas, labels, beliefs, doctrine and all that hoopla is reality.

Let us grow up and move beyond this trap. Let us understand that thought is not truth. Let us understand that truth is not a product of the mind. Truth is independent of the mind. It is the pure and simple fact of the reality of something. It is the way things actually are.

> *"The heart of the matter is that we are living in a culture which has been hypnotized with symbols—words, numbers, measures, qualities and images—and we mistake them for, and prefer them to, physical reality. We believe that the proof of the pudding is in the chemical analysis, not in the eating."*
>
> —Alan Watts, *Does It Matter?*

So if truth is not thought then how can we come to know the truth?

Well, once again, it's so obvious that we miss it: Truth can only be experienced.

TRUTH AND EXPERIENCE

Consider the life of young children. If we look at young children before the age of 5 we will notice that their minds are not yet fully developed, yet their capacity to fully experience is there. Children that have not been too traumatized are fully present and completely engaged in life. They are 'being themselves to fullness'. When they encounter a new person or experience something for the first time, they approach it in an expanded state of openness, wonder and excitement. When they are happy, they are fully happy and when they are hurt, they fully express their emotions and, if allowed, release the emotion until it is exhausted. They flow with life, taking in life as it is and letting it go, with only the memory remaining and with no residual resistance or charge attached. Only later, as children grow up, does the analyzing capacity of the mind come into being.

When that capacity arises, the mind, in its self-reflecting nature, starts to separate itself from the experience and begins to categorize and organize the experience by associating past similar people, places and things. Over time, as the storehouse of memories and associations build-up, the child can access this memory bank and reflect back on past pleasant or unpleasant experiences to make beneficial choices in the future.

But what comes first? The experience of reality must come first. If there is no experience then there is no material to draw on to organize. Therefore, there is no thought. So, in a way, the mind's purpose is similar to the purpose of our digestive system: to assimilate in a non-physical way our perceptions of life . . . but the food or experience must come first. And just as we cannot live on imaginary or already digested food, so, too, we cannot exist just on thought, which is merely a processed experience.

As we contemplate this, what becomes clear is: our experience needs to be pure, unfiltered and uninterrupted. This is where true fulfillment occurs. If we are sitting on the beach watching the sunset with a loved one, it is only satisfying to the degree that we let the whole experience in. We are being fully ourselves in the event. We are taking in the occasion to its completeness. There is a pristine and pure quality without anything mixed in by our perceptions. We let in the experience, be with it and let it out. Let in, let be and let go is the mantra of experiencing.

Jesus said that if you are to enter the kingdom of heaven you must be as a little child. When you meet an enlightened person, you get the sense of immense wisdom but also inspiring innocence. The enlightened interact with the world as it is. They see you in the divinity that you are. They have contacted reality, experienced its fullness without anything getting in the way. They see the truth . . . the way things actually are and as a result they act in harmony with the reality of your essence.

If there is nothing standing in the way between reality and ourselves, then our perceptions of Self, life and others is clear. Then the mind can take this complete experience and do its job of organizing it so that the individual can make wise choices in the future. If our experience is incomplete and half-digested, the mind has limited material to organize for fuller living. Just as a jury cannot make a determination on incomplete evidence, so too the individual cannot make wise choices based on incomplete or muddied experience.

Now this is the problem that most spiritual paths have been tackling for centuries: how to free us from our sense of separation, how to help us to fully experience the divine gift of existence that's our own personal life.

Through the ages, numerous spiritual techniques have been devised to meet this challenge. I have tested many of these techniques and I have observed many others attempting to apply them to their lives. And in my experience, spiritual disciplines often fail to deliver the desired results, not because their techniques are ineffective or faulty, but because they do not take into account what it is that actually blocks us from fully experiencing reality in the first place.

For example, if an auto-mechanic does not perform a complete diagnosis of a problem with your vehicle, he will probably fail to correctly fix it. He may even end up fixing a problem that did not exist and thereby create another problem. Similarly, if a spiritual tradition aimed at correcting a human condition fails to take into account a diagnosis of how that human condition arose, then ultimately that tradition will fail to help people find liberation. In fact, it may even create further bondage.

So we must investigate and come to an understanding of what blocks us from experiencing the truth or the way things actually are.

Once again, with great respect to your own wisdom and investigation, I'd like to offer a suggestion for you to consider: two of the major roadblocks on the path of spiritual awakening are Trauma and Socialization.

CHAPTER 4

MAJOR BLOCKS TO AWAKENING

TRAUMA
Being overwhelmed

I define trauma as "an overwhelming experience which we could not fully get through or process given our ability at the time of the incident(s)". We all have trauma. There are just different degrees of it. No one is really free of it in life. Trauma can come from any type of event. It can entail any degree of severity, from being physically abused to witnessing a pet run over, to living with a critical parent for 18 years, to a momentary angry glance from a teacher we admired. It can be a sudden event or an ongoing difficult situation. It could be the result of continual neglect or abandonment. It could be the result of an injury, a surgery or the stress of moving from one culture to another.

The main characteristic is that it is overwhelming for us at the time. It results from our encountering a situation (usually but not always when we are young) in which we were confronted with an experience of something or someone too difficult to handle. We feared that if we totally let in the event that it would destroy us, so we held back the part of the experience that was too much for us.

If there were others who were related to the event, we may have suppressed whatever communications we needed to make to them but couldn't. We perhaps lacked the verbal skills necessary to be understood. This could have been the result of others suppressing our communications either by punishing us, ignoring us, or not being present. These uncompleted communications to others associated with the event(s) could carry an emotional charge for us—the charge being anger, fear, grief, guilt, anxiety, rage, sadness, or any other emotion that arose as we were immersed in the situation. These feelings were too difficult to communicate to the parent, friend, teacher or abuser. It may not have been safe to tell the truth of our feelings to these people. We may have known intuitively that they were actually hurt themselves and just couldn't hear our pain. It might have been too overwhelming, in turn, for them to receive our communication. We didn't know how to say: "That hurts" or "I need you to listen to me", "I am a real person just like you", "understand me", "I exist here", "I want you to love me". So we resisted the experience and held back what we really needed to say.

If the event occurred in childhood, our normal open and expansive nature started to contract. We pulled back our full engagement in the world and froze. We did the only thing we could do at the time, the second best thing . . . hold back our radiance and be other than who we really are.

In order to protect ourselves from the overwhelming experience, we decided to behave differently than our authentic selves and to take on a particular belief about life, others or ourselves. In so doing, we cemented ourselves into a set pattern of behaviour and fixed beliefs that we continually superimposed onto reality.

The end result is that we withdrew partially from life and began to live more and more in our minds or in thought. Instead of openly engaging in life, the trauma caused us to recoil, freeze, and become hyper-vigilant and keep life at a safe distance. We acted as if we were trying to figure life out first, before living it.

This stuck state is what I call "the reactive mind". It is composed of all the overwhelming experiences, the incomplete communications to others, the erroneous beliefs we have made up about Self, life and others and all the ensuing emotions, thoughts and experiences that are associated with these original experiences.

This stuck state is similar to a large battery. The battery is solid and substantial, yet it has an energetic charge. Likewise, it's as if we experience life from the point of view of the battery. When we meet situations and people that were similar to the past overpowering event, the energetic charge of our battery is released in inappropriate over—or under-reactivity, thus causing us to create further havoc and negative karma in our lives.

BEN'S STORY

A good example of all this is a client I worked with in a one-to-one session called Clearing. Ben grew-up with a depressed and judgmental mother who was a survivor of a Jewish concentration camp in WW2. His mother never recovered from her experience and lived life from the belief that life is terrible suffering. Ben's joyful exuberance was too much for his mother and she was frequently critical of his expressions of happiness or pleasure. His natural zest for life challenged her negative beliefs and she reacted by coming down hard on him. His response was to shut down his inherent happiness.

Ben did not understand why his mother behaved the way she did toward him. He was too young to possess the verbal capacity to express what he was going through and tell his mother how her behaviour affected him. But all of these incomplete communications became stored in his memory. Because they were associated with feelings of great distress, he pushed them deep down into unconsciousness in order to distance himself from the pain.

As he grew and developed an ego, he incorporated these unconscious beliefs and feelings into his own self identity and developed a deeply held stuck state that said it was his own being that was at fault, not his mother. He ill-logically decided that it was because he was unlovable that his mother's reactions to him were so unloving. As a result of this decision about his identity, he came up with a false solution: to only be good or nice or loving, to express only what was socially acceptable, as an outer compensation for his perceived inner defect.

But by taking on the point of view of being unlovable, Ben ended up perceiving himself through a lens that cast a dark colour of unloveableness on all the bright spots of his being. And, despite his desperate attempts to prove his worth by acting in ways acceptable to his mother, he was unable to heal his inner sense of unlovableness and help his mother heal her inner wound. And because doing-ness is in a different universe from being, which does not transform the sense of identity, over time his self-loathing increased.

Just like any human being, Ben made mistakes but he was only able to recognize the behaviours that validated his "I'm unlovable" theme. He overlooked any actions that were not consistent with this belief. Behind his outer presentation of "being nice", he sank deeper and deeper into self-dislike and this perception came to be mirrored by others. He attracted others who criticized and mistreated him just as his mother had done in his earlier years. The emotional charge associated with all the uncompleted communications to his mother began to seep into his close relationships and his over reactivity resulted in relationships full of struggle and turmoil. He blamed others for treating him in uncaring ways, thus re-creating the victim/ perpetrator game he had with his mother. Ben created the same story that he had experienced in childhood, though with different actors, it was the same drama.

Guilt and self-shaming then set in. By mistreating others out of his unconscious reactivity, he became mired in a negative cycle of guilt and shame that reinforced his sense of not being lovable by saying to himself: "Well I do bad things therefore I am a bad person and I deserve to suffer". His life had become like his mother's: hard like cement, all mixed up and permanently set.

Fortunately in the work that Ben did in the Clearing sessions, he was able to go back to the origin of his "I'm unlovable" decision. He imagined his mother as being present in the session, completed his communications to her and uncovered for himself the reality that he was born as a magnificent divine being who had become innocently trapped in an erroneous belief about himself.

Ben's story illustrates something that is common to most of us. At some point in our lives, as a result of some kind of trauma, we withdrew from full involvement in life and began to see ourselves, life and others as if through a tinted glass casing imprinted with our manufactured pictures of reality. From a distance, we inspected life, Self and others and expected them to all conform to our beliefs based on what we had concluded from this past trauma. No matter which way we turned inside this shell, we gazed out at the world through these illusions.

It can be said that our experience of the world is intimately connected with the particular point of view that we have adopted. In this mental state, seeing is not believing. It is more accurate to say that believing is seeing. We project our internal pictures onto reality and that's what we see. The internal pictures are the composite meanings of everything we have made up and constructed around all the experiences we have had in our personal history. Even our senses are altered by the mind (as we saw in the chair exercise). We see what we believe and then take what we see to further confirm our beliefs and then see more of that. It's a vicious circle. The glass casing is our reactive mind, the buffer between Self and reality, formed when reality is too hard to experience.

To summarize, following a traumatic experience or set of experiences, we suspend our reactions, pull back from life, make up a negative belief about ourselves or others (to explain why the event occurred) and behave in ways that are consistent with the negative belief. Out of these beliefs we create actions that are destructive to our relationships and end up feeling guilty, ashamed and undeserving of good things in life. These negative expectations then attract victimizing behaviours from others which reinforce our beliefs and feelings in a feedback loop . . . a vicious recurring cycle. And as the joy of life is a function of fully experiencing life, our happiness becomes compromised. Since the awareness of truth is a function of our contact with reality, by spending more and more time in our minds or in beliefs about reality, rather than reality itself, we become more deluded and unhappy.

> *"Every time an external event reminds you of something in the past, you begin to experience the past . . . Your reactions are automatic, habitual, unconscious and pre-programmed. So if you do not work through and bring it to a conclusion it will continually repeat itself until it reaches a conclusion"*
>
> —Amrit Desai—*Voyage to Betterment*

SOCIALIZATION
Mass Hypnosis

Layered within these overwhelming experiences is our mass cultural environment: the sociological influences of our society, religious upbringing, peers, neighborhood, workplace, etc., as well. Within these are a composite of many viewpoints, concepts, attitudes and behaviour patterns that have caused us to see and interact with the world in pre-programmed ways. Most of these are unconsciously acquired. We are born as magnificent, pure, shining beings into the world; we are then shaped, molded, programmed, impressed, branded, or forced into being other than what we are through the process of socialization. We lose touch with our true essence and learn very quickly that it's better to fit into another mould rather than fit with our selves.

21

Being socialized into a particular cultural environment is like being a novice actor on a stage with other seasoned actors who are performing in an elaborate play. We must learn our lines and acquire our roles from others who have come from generations of actors before us. However, no one knows what the drama is leading to. No one understands the purpose of the play. We all assume the older actors know. And very few of us are courageousness enough to break the illusion of the play and ask: "Why are we acting? What is this play all about?" We do not think to burst the bubble of make-believe and look behind the curtain or into the audience and find out what real life is all about.

In reality, we are not prisoners of anyone in life. We are trapped in our minds by accepting the programming of how to see the world and ourselves. Through observation and training, we have concluded that others know the true way of living and we imitate the behaviour and assumptions behind the way they see the world. We shape ourselves like chameleons in order to be accepted and loved. We are the ones that have not questioned this programming. We are totally unaware that we have done this to ourselves. Had we been placed, as young children, in a different culture, in a different family or a different country, we would have grown up acting differently with a markedly different perspective of life. But we would still be trapped in our minds.

I once had a stark realization of this when I met a Chinese man who grew up in Jamaica. He had a Jamaican accent but was from Asian descent. In addition, he was a Zen Buddhist (a traditionally Japanese tradition), he played the sitar (an Indian tradition) and he was gay. He was a mixture of many different stereotypes and I kept trying to pigeon-hole his behaviour into one of these. But he didn't fit any of them. My mind was totally blown. The only thing I could do was to try to get to know him and relate to him as he actually was—which is the way we all want to be related to anyways.

A major contribution to our socialization is the media and advertising. Advertisers have spent millions of dollars of research money learning how to convince people to buy their products through subtle manipulation. It is estimated that people are exposed to an average of 40,000 commercials a year—2,800,000 over a lifetime. According to A.C. Neilson Co., children are exposed to over 8,000 commercials a year for junk food and only 165 for healthy food. The effectiveness of this advertising is evident in the fact that there are now more overweight adults in the USA than normal weight adults. Add to this picture the time that we spend plugged into our iPods and cell phones and we begin to realize how little time we spend in reality, in being with the world the way it actually is.

In a sense, we live in a state of mass hypnosis. It is a misconception that we are only subject to hypnotic suggestion when we lose consciousness or fall asleep watching the hypnotist's pendulum. We are subject to suggestion anytime we relax, get into a zoned out state, or focus on something for an extended period of time. Does this not describe exactly what happens when we watch TV? We are mass programmed with hundreds of messages a day to not be our natural selves and to find our fulfillment outside ourselves in the thousands of consumer products advertised. Each one of these products eventually changes, degrades, gets damaged, decays and ends up in the landfill site. We are trapped in the temporary exhilaration of acquisition and the subsequent grief of loss. Our world is polluted with these illusions of consumer happiness as we overlook our real source of fulfillment: the connection to ourselves—the connection we lost as children. Therefore we do not exist in a natural authentic state of consciousness. Our everyday state of consciousness is actually an altered state attached to our erroneous expectations of the outer world. We are deluded into thinking that this state is normal, but normal only means a state of hypnosis shared by everyone else. Just because we share the same delusion does not mean it is real.

> *"If you do something enough times, the subconscious mind begins to believe that this behavior pattern is what you want and therefore stores it for you and makes it part of your natural behaviour."*
>
> —Tom Nicholi, Master Hypnotist

Many years ago I had an alarming and comical cosmic experience of the power of belief in creating a reality that did not exist. It led me into contemplating the power of masses of people holding the same belief. The implications were illuminating and at the same time alarming.

THE TWITS OF SAINT TWINKLE

In the 1970's I was living in a co-op house with some friends. We were pursuing a healthy, spiritual lifestyle and exploring all manner of new-age practices and philosophies. There was an explosion of this across North America. It seemed that everyone and his grandmother was coming up with some new belief system and healing modality. Just as a joke, and perhaps as a disguised cynical comment on all of this, one of the residents of the house and I decided to start our own religion. We called it "Twinklism".

We created a Saint of Twinklism called Saint Twinkle. Saint Twinkle was an animated 5-pointed star with two eyes, a nose, a smiley mouth, and seven rays of light emanating outward. We designated Saint Twinkle as the Patron Saint of Joy and Enlightenment. We were his disciples. We called ourselves the "Twits of Saint Twinkle" and we each fashioned a sacred garment for worship, which was a large paper bag with eyeholes and a nose cut out. We drew a picture of our holy master on the bag just above the eyeholes (of course where the third eye was) and placed it on our head. We had a holy relic (a beer nut) and a sacred elixir (beer) that we had to drink before any ceremony with him/her (being new-agey politically correct, the saint had no sexual orientation). Since this was going to be a secret society we decided upon a secret greeting to indicate our membership. We would extend our arms out towards each other and point our index finger back at ourselves and touch our fists together and say: "who-r-u", indicating our deep commitment to self-discovery. Since Saint

Twinkle was the Saint of Joyousness and Enlightenment, the goal of the spiritual path was to open up our 'Clown Chakra'.

We would put on our sacred garment, the paper bag, and go into a darkened room and light a candle. We would start off meditating quietly in a mock solemnity and then just laugh whenever we felt like it. Of course it was very easy to laugh because what we were doing was so hilarious to begin with. We always felt good after drinking the sacred beer and paying homage to the holy beer nut and laughing ourselves half to death.

We did this a number of times and decided once again, just as a joke, that we were going to present our new religion to the world. There was a protest rally against the Vietnam War and we thought that since there were a lot of other philosophical societies and religious groups in the protest, we felt we needed a representation there as well. We put our sacred paper bags over our heads and walked in the parade, occasionally chanting: "Make bags not bombs, Make bags not bombs." A few people asked us what we were doing and we told them. Some people got the joke but a lot of people thought we were nuts. We just pretended that they were crazy and that we were of course of a much higher vibration than them, being the chosen ones of Saint Twinkle.

This hilarity continued for a few months and at one point in the meditation I decided that since channeling was finding its way into the new-age, I would try my hand at channeling Saint Twinkle, once again just as a joke. I would go into a meditation after we both chanted "Ohm silly mahn. Ohm silly mahn" and communicate in a far-off, spaced-out tone, some inane esoteric things about life on the seventh plane of some made-up non-physical realm.

But at some point something changed and I began to have a vague feeling that Saint Twinkle was actually there. I would put my attention on him/her and feel the presence and receive some guidance. Remarkably the guidance was quite cogent to my life. I began to feel the presence more often throughout the day as I went through my normal activities. Then one day, something happened that changed everything.

I was traveling on the subway one morning. I was feeling very down about my life, how it was going nowhere, I didn't seem to be getting what I wanted out of life, I was a loser, etc. The whole thing. At one point, I had to close my eyes to hide my tears from the other passengers. Suddenly a vision of Saint Twinkle appeared in my mind. The Saint was radiating light and appeared suspended just in front of me and was mocking me with a very sad face and a tongue hanging down with the message: "Be happy, this is only temporary".

I was shocked at how clear the image and how palpable the vision was. I was also shocked at how something Ralph and I had both made up became so real. I began to wonder about belief systems and religions. If just two of us were able to create something that we could actually experience and communicate to out of nothing, knowing full well that it was not real from the start, what did that suggest about thousands or millions of so-called "believers"? Are they experiencing phenomena that are real or is it simply a mass hallucination created by huge numbers of people putting their attention on the same thing? Did my friend and I create a false experience but were subsequently contacted by an actual angelic being appearing in the form as Saint Twinkle in a form that we could accept? I do not know.

To this day, my experience of Saint Twinkle amazes and puzzles me. At the time, it was a major epiphany to realize the extent of the psychological forces that condition and imprison so many of us on the planet. I let go of the Saint Twinkle joke. The joke ended up being on us! But it helped me realize the double-edged sword of religious dogma. We are not only the prisoner but also the jailer, imprisoned by our own device, limited by what does not exist. The insanity of it all was hilarious but also alarmingly painful. That backfiring joke changed my life!

It was then that I made it my life-long aspiration to experience the truth for myself, independent of any fabricated belief system. It is that commitment that still motivates me, years later, to assist and encourage others to go beyond belief to the truth itself and to not settle for anything less.

This whole story elicits a number of questions:

If as the result of our personal history including our socialization, we are not fully experiencing reality, then how do we see what is true beyond our ego?

If our perceptions are limited and can be influenced by what we believe, then how do we experience the universal truth which is outside our minds?

If (as we explored earlier) the spiritual path is all about living from the truth, then how can we know the truth so that we can live from it?

And finally, how does the spiritual teacher, spiritual master or guru fit into the picture?

I have thought long and hard on these questions. In a sense, my whole life has been devoted to an examination of these. What I am presenting here is a number of suggestions for how you might start answering these questions. The important thing is that you examine these questions for yourself. Let us look at some methods for going beyond belief to the truth itself, looking at the limitations of each of these as we go along.

CHAPTER 5

MISTAKEN METHODS OF KNOWING ULTIMATE TRUTH

THE SCIENTIFIC METHOD
Measuring God

The universal scientific method involves five steps:

1. Formulating a question concerning a particular aspect of reality, based on the knowledge already available to us.
2. Developing a hypothesis, using information that is already known or accepted, that predicts what will happen if we put our question to the test.
3. Constructing an experiment designed to test the hypothesis using observable data.
4. Analyzing the empirical, or observed, data from the experiment to see if it confirms our hypothesis or not.
5. Communicating and discussing the results of our experiment and then constructing a theory verified by similar results repeated over time.

Through the scientific method scientists have discovered many of the accepted truths of the physical world. The problem with the scientific method is that it is limited to the study of observable, objective data, of which many are independent isolated events. Anything that is outside these events that could influence these events is not considered or may be overlooked.

Scientists are limited to the sensitivity of their measuring instruments and although measuring devices are able to detect finer and finer gradations of physical reality, even to the subatomic level, they cannot analyze the subjective components of a person's reality. Science has difficulty studying anything it cannot calibrate. Quantum physics, which looks at the interaction between energy and matter, comes close, with many of its theories approximating the esoteric philosophy of ancient spiritual texts, but it is still not there yet. And generally, Western science limits itself to the examination of objective, observable data that ignores the inner dimension of subjective experience. As such science has its limitations.

AUTHORITY, TRADITION, CONSENSUS AND APPEARANCE
What the herd heard is the word

Often people infer that authority figures know the truth because they have many students or they are associated with an age-old lineage of an established practice and esoteric philosophy. Maybe there is a consensus among thousands of people that these teachers know the truth. Maybe the teacher looks and acts the part: long beard, white robe and slow, hypnotic speech. However, they may simply be reiterating material that they have been taught, rather than speaking from their own experience. They may be teaching techniques that are actually harmful. (For example, I once heard of a guru who taught that the way to remove negative thoughts was to bang your head against a wall exactly 144 times. This may actually work by giving you a headache that distracts you from your negative self-talk!)

Modern history is scattered with the debris of hundreds or thousands of followers of charismatic leaders who heard all the right things and believed the leaders knew the truth because everyone else thought they did. Authority, tradition, consensus and appearance are not proof that someone knows the truth, only proof that a lot of people believe they do!

INDIVIDUAL PERCEPTION
It is what I see, you see?

We perceive the objective world through our five senses. According to a commonly held belief, "seeing is believing". However, the information received through the senses is a second-hand experience of reality because it is mediated by the senses. If the camera you are using to record the light patterns of a particular object has flaws in its internal structure, then the image you record will have these flaws.

It is important to realize that most of our senses operate within a certain range of vibration. For instance we can only hear the sounds that are within the human spectrum of hearing. Vibrations that occur above and below this range are imperceptible to us. Dogs and cats can hear sound frequencies outside of the human range. Our vision is restricted to the range between infrared and ultraviolet. In addition, our depth or distance perception of sight and sound has limitations. Owls and eagles, for instance, can hear finer subtleties of sound at a greater distance than we can. So we are not getting the full compliment of experience of reality and therefore not fully perceiving reality. If this is so, how can we know if we know the truth?

It is also important to understand that physical perception occurs by means of a complex set of intermediary events, never directly. For example, in visual perception, light energy impinges on the eye, travels through the lens of the eye, impinges on the retinal cells, is translated into weak electrical charges, and relayed to the brain. All perception involves some kind of process even before it reaches the brain. The brain then associates these electrical impressions with similar ones that are stored in the memory and then we recognize it as a chair. The sensations all occur through a conduit of physical responses, memory accessing and interpretation. Any break, disability or malfunction in the system can produce an error. If there are problems with the retina, we can get a distorted image and not see the chair accurately so then the brain can interpret it as something else. As far as mental perceptions are concerned, the chair exercise described above provides proof of the fact that we are capable of creating a sense of something real simple through the process of thought. These abilities are under both conscious and unconscious control.

Individual perception is indirect. There is the sensation here and the Self over there. There is a separation between the perception and the perceiver, and a process bridging the gap. There is a pathway between the two but there is no union with them. So although there is a certain amount of reality that we can perceive with our senses, we cannot guarantee all of what we see, hear, touch, taste and smell is accurate.

AFFIRMATION, POSITIVE THINKING AND VISUALIZATION
Fake it 'til you make it, even though you make it fake

Teachings abound on the subject of positive affirmation. The general practice is to begin with a statement that a person wishes to be true about him or herself or life and declare this over and over again. Through the process of repetition the person perceives a mental and emotional shift and feels more positive and more energetic.

The shift is really about moving thought around in the mind, emphasizing one type of thought to the exclusion of the others and creating a new perception, much like what Ralph and I did with the Twits of Saint Twinkle. We may affirm that "I am a wonderful radiant light being" and there may be an element of truth to our affirmation. But what if it isn't true? If it isn't, then we are just adding another delusion to our set of deluded beliefs.

Positive affirmations have a place in bolstering self-esteem and increasing a sense of positive orientation to the self. But they do not have a place in our goal of knowing the truth of who we are. We are just taking what we want to be true and through the process of reinforcement, building an experience of ourselves that matches the way we want to feel. In fact, many spiritual teachers substitute positive affirmations for the truth. After years and years of stating the same belief system over and over, students may begin to have spiritual experiences consistent with the dogma, but it does not mean that they have discovered the truth itself. In addition, their experiences may become limited to the parameters of the dogma that they are exposed to. If they do have a deeper realization, they may reject it. Oftentimes, the goal of the particular spiritual path, whether it is the experience of non-self, the void, non-duality or cosmic consciousness, determines the kind of spiritual experiences people have.

LOGIC
Fundamentally mental

Logic is an intellectual process that consists of one or more premises and a conclusion. A premise is a statement that is offered in support of a claim being made. Premises and claims can be either true or false. In the process of logic one presents an argument to prove something to be true or false. One begins with a statement or a premise that one knows is true and adds in other statements that are known to be true to arrive at a third statement or conclusion which is said to be logically deducible from the prior statements. For example, one can say that some philosophers are Platonists; some mathematicians are philosophers; therefore, some mathematicians are Platonists. This is a sequence that comes to a logical conclusion. For logic to operate, one must be sure that the component statements are in fact true. If they are not, then one can come to a false conclusion.

In many ways, logic limits its concern to the task of verifying a truth rather than discovering truth itself. It must first of all begin with premises that are already known to be true. For instance, I can say that science has proven that the physical universe is composed of energy. My body is part of the physical universe. Therefore I am energy. This may seem like a logical statement and entirely valid. In fact, many spiritual seekers have made this erroneous conclusion. However there is an assumption that my identity is physical or that who I am is physical.

As stated, the problem with logic is that it must start with premises that are known to be true. There are a limited amount of concepts that we know are true and so our use of logic is necessarily limited to those concepts. As well, logic is limited to the intellect and we have seen that the mind can only take the elements of experience it knows to be true and organize them. It cannot know the ultimate truth because it does not have the ultimate experience within it as a premise to start with, therefore it cannot prove or disprove anything related to the ultimate truth.

> *"We may learn things by (1) hearsay or on authority; (2) by the mere suggestion of experience; (3) by reasoning; (4) or by immediate and complete perception . . . this last mode of knowing proceeds from an adequate knowing of the absolute nature of things."*
> —Benedict Spinoza from *Cosmic Conscious*
> by Maurice Buck

OCCULT AND PSYCHIC REVELATIONS
Inner sensing beyond the outer

Many people can have profound experiences of leaving the body and going into other realms, of hearing deceased loved ones or divine beings speak to them, of seeing visions of celestial worlds, of hearing an inner voice relaying impressions or intuitions about others and themselves, of feeling energetic releases, of viewing scenes of past lives, etc. These extraordinary occurrences happen to sensitive people frequently on the spiritual path and are not unusual. Important insights can be gained from these experiences that can transform and inform our lives.

But people can get trapped in wanting more and more of these experiences, thinking that they represent a spiritual realm of ultimate truth. These experiences are not to be discounted but they should be distinguished from ultimate truth. They point to a finer, subtler realm than the physical world perceived not by the outer senses but by the inner senses of psychic seeing, hearing, touch, feeling, etc. These are much like the outer senses but are focused inward to a subtler space.

It is certainly important to cultivate our ability to "look within" but we should also realize that these inner senses can be deceiving just as they can be accurate. This inner world is much more fluid and amorphous and as such is subject to more interpretation. It takes more skill and considerable training for individuals to work within these realms to distinguish what is real from what is subject to the mind's influence. Although there is significant learning in these realms and great wisdom that can inform and uplift our lives, many spiritual seekers can get waylaid in this territory thinking that the ultimate truth of self, life and others is found here.

It is important to note that the process of "sensing" is operational here, with the same complex of intermediary events. Just as our outer senses are subject to manipulation by our beliefs, so too are our inner ones. It is still in the realm of indirect experience.

DOGMA DOO-DOO
Somebody Else's Answers

We have talked earlier about how thought is just a description of truth and that the mind can only experience thought and not experience reality.

Basically, dogma is somebody else's thoughts, packaged and organized into a set of concepts, theories or stories. At best, dogma is supported by logic but often it is not. We might say that dogma is a fixed set of second-hand beliefs promoted by a guru or teacher on a spiritual path that we believe is a first-hand description of reality. We accept it because the dogma appears to fill in all the empty holes in our understanding and appeases the uncomfortableness of our 'not knowing'. It saves us from having to put the effort into finding the truth for ourselves. We might say it is the lazy way out. In many cases, dogma is based on someone's authentic mystical experience, so it comes with a sense of authority. Often times, if the teacher is part of a tradition or lineage, the teacher's genuine spiritual experience may be mixed in with the dogma and communicated within the context, language and jargon of the accepted teachings, so that the mixture has a ring of irrefutableness. In the face of this seeming certainty, we willingly suspend our disbelief and take on the teacher's description (or menu) as reality (the food).

Even if the teacher is fully enlightened and is communicating the way reality actually is, it still has to be translated into language or a representation and cannot be fully transmitted. A picture is still a picture. The map is not the territory. A model of reality, no matter how accurate in detail, is still a reasonable facsimile.

Over time as the dogma is repeated over and over again, we become indoctrinated into believing that the teacher's first-hand experience is our first-hand experience. In fact, it is a belief system that is second-hand and could very well be 3rd-or 4th—or 22nd—hand if the teacher is just as caught up in presenting the dogma that was passed down through his/her lineage.

"Filling the mind with all the highest spiritual teachings will not lead to liberation. Forget all you know, observe your experience and freedom will follow."
—Wayne Liquorman, *Eastern Mystics*

Many dogmatic spiritual paths are faith-based. We are persuaded to accept the point of view of existence on faith alone. We are extolled that we must believe first, we must first have faith, we must trust, we must set aside our doubts and confusion and take on a pre-digested way of seeing life, God, love, ourselves and others in order to know the truth. "Believe what is written first and then you will come to know." But we really don't come to know the truth through this path of faith. We only come to know what someone else says is the truth.

There is a certain value in accepting things on faith. Faith can create openness to new experience and counteracts an attitude of cynical disbelief. But faith often extends into blind faith where one goes to the extreme of becoming open to believing only what the authority figure says is true. As we become fully indoctrinated into the belief system, we may have some insights from time to time that seem like they are genuine, but in reality they are just like vowels in a *Scrabble* game. We move them around, up and down, to create different combinations of the dogma, but the basic elements are still all the same. There is a sense of novelty that comes from moving things around, but in reality there is nothing new.

THE DANGER OF DOGMA

The danger of dogma is three-fold:

1. It limits the realm of our spiritual experience to the boundaries prescribed by the dogma.

2. It can create false experiences that appear to be real.
3. It opens us up to cult indoctrination and all the abuses of fundamentalism.

Limits of Dogma

Let us begin with the first danger. If we take on someone else's second-hand belief as our first-hand experience, then it becomes a point of view, a way of seeing reality rather than an experience of reality. We use that point of view of the dogma as a reference point to measure and evaluate further ideas and experiences. These are rejected, manipulated or re-shaped by the mind to fit into the dogmatic framework.

The tragedy here is that a person can only go as far in their spiritual development as the dogma can take them and then they will cease to make progress. Once they get stuck, the only sense of progress they feel comes from the continual re-enforcement of, or addition to, their dogma. But this is just re-arranging and re-connecting the content of the mind and feeling some effects. Eventually their spiritual path becomes dull and boring and they need more dogma to feel a sense of newness.

Jill's self-deception

Jill, a woman who attended one of my retreats, was part of a belief system that strongly maintained that the Self did not exist. At one point on the retreat, she began to enter into a divine experience in which she perceived not only divine love but also perceived herself as being divine love. As she began relating her direct experience she began to radiate from that divine state. However, as soon as she recognized that her direct experience contradicted the dogma of her teacher, she backed away from her experience. She could not let go of the belief in the non-existence of Self and at the same time be divine love. Her direct realization challenged the engrained structure of her dogma and for her to be in direct experience she would have had to let go of that structure and also disagree with her teacher.

Instead, she chose the security of that structure rather than dwell in her true nature. She fell out of union with her divine being. This was a tragedy to herself and to all others who she would have met in life who could have been touched by that radiance of love.

False Experience

The second aspect of a dogmatic approach is that we can easily create erroneous experiences out of dogma and believe them to be true even though they have been self-created. This is a common dynamic well-known in the field of cognitive psychology in which an individual who takes on a particular inner point of view about objects or people will actually outwardly impose that point of view on those events and experience sensations and perceptions that did not in fact occur but are consistent with that point of view.

During my work at a retreat centre years ago, I witnessed a spiritual teacher who taught a particular concept of human awakening and described in detail to his students all the feelings, characteristics and perceptions that he had in this experience. He then guided them through a meditation in which they were told they would experience his same level of cosmic consciousness and invariably every student reported an experience that conformed exactly to his experiences. All the students were impressed by the great teachings and techniques of this master. However, it was clearly apparent that the experience they had was completely manufactured in their minds to conform to the teacher's belief system.

The trap here is that many spiritual seekers, out of faith in a dogma, can actually create or impose upon genuine spiritual experience phenomena that do not exist. They may then proceed in their lives thinking they have had divine illumination. And when a genuine opportunity for direct spiritual experience comes along, they will by-pass it, thinking that they have already achieved awakening when it was just manufactured in their own mind.

Fundamentalism and Cults

The third pitfall in accepting dogma is the possibility of indoctrination into a cult, often resulting in abuses of sexual, physical, emotional and monetary exploitation. Most spiritual practice expands our consciousness and opens us up mentally and emotionally. We can let go of our normal defenses and in that expanded state where there is greater inner aliveness and heart presence, we can ignore our intuition that something is not right. If we have not worked through enough of our personal trauma issues, our personal boundaries may be weak and we can become susceptible to manipulation from charismatic individuals. Often, individuals who get caught in a cult have a prior history of abusive relationships. They may be looking for the ideal father or mother in the spiritual leader. They may be looking to the spiritual community for a sense of family and familial love and security that they never had as a child. When they find it in the leader and the spiritual family gathered around the leader, they will do almost anything to keep it. Sadly, some spiritual leaders can have a sociopathic or narcissistic personality and can exploit their students by making them feel special or more advanced than others or the rest of society. The sociological pressure within such a group to conform can be manipulated to the point where people will do almost anything to be in the dysfunctional "family".

It is important to be aware of the characteristics of a cult so that you can recognize them and avoid such a group. To be forewarned is to be forearmed. Here are some common aspects of a cult:

1. Unquestioning adherence to a set ideology or philosophy as the ultimate truth, which must be taken on by faith and not questioned.

2. Zealous admiration, subservience and commitment to a self-appointed, "absolutely certain", charismatic leader who claims to have a special spiritual illumination or divine gift and demands loyalty (sometimes through several lifetimes) and dictates the behaviour of his/her members.

3. Exalted status of the group, the leader and the ideology that claims that they are the "only way" to the salvation of Self or humanity.

4. Perception of the leader as perfect and unaccountable for his/her actions. Any actions that are reprehensible are considered as above reproach or as some divine teaching lessons to the person or group. Any criticalness of the leader is turned back on the students as "projections" of their own lack of higher consciousness.

5. Justification of any unethical or immoral means as a necessary end to promote the advancement of the group and its bogus goal to uplift humanity.

6. Heavy coercion and pressure to devote excessive time, money and effort to group activities, especially fund-raising and the recruiting of new members to the point where people ignore their inner voice and engage in activities that they normally would not.

7. Control and manipulation of members through shame, group dynamics, hypnotic techniques, alienation, sleep deprivation, over-work, shunning, etc.

8. Use of special language, dress, symbols, jargon, etc., which only have a special meaning to those within the group.

9. A belief and fear that the world outside the group is somehow dangerous and tainted and that the only way to salvation is to be separate from the world or socialize only with group members.

10. Clone-like behaviour of group members who behave, dress and speak the same.

Not all of the criteria need to be met to indicate the existence of a cult. One or two of these can. It is an interesting exercise to use the above characteristics of a cult, to scrutinize any existent group, organization, religion, political party, business or even a country. If we did this, we would be amazed to find major or minor cults everywhere.

Think of the Al Qaeda in Afghanistan, the Spanish Inquisition, the Confederate States, Nazi Germany, just to name a few. What was the basis of all of these cults? Indoctrination into a dogma! The dogma of the superior Aryan race, the dogma that Jews are evil and need to be destroyed, the dogma that women using herbs to heal in the middle ages are witches, the dogma that men and women of a different colour are inferior and therefore can be enslaved, the dogma that if I carry a bomb and explode it in a crowded marketplace, I will go to heaven, the dogma that it's okay to lie about weapons of mass destruction to invade a country because I am bringing democracy there, the dogma that the end always justifies the means. How many wars have been caused by dogma, where one country in the name of God fought another who also had God on their side? The pattern repeats itself throughout the ages. It seems that it's brand-new history, same old news. Everyone has God standing up for them! Why won't the real God just sit down!

The Tragedy of Dogma

The tragedy is that we don't kill one another out of the truth; we kill one another out of a facsimile of truth, a shadow, a chimera, out of lies, out of something that does not exist. We destroy one another for nothing. This is absolutely incredibly insane. This is beyond tragedy. If we let the insanity of all of this in, it would shatter us. We would fall to the floor and cry out in despair. We would yell out to the world in a rage that we hope would shatter the ice around all the hearts of those who have destroyed their neighbors because they held different beliefs. The differences were only in their minds, not their hearts. If we could only sit down and have tea across the table from the enemy that we have been socialized to believe is evil and ask them what their life is like, we would discover a "common folk" similar to us. We would discover someone who wants a good life for their family, who wants to make a contribution to the world, who wants to love and be loved. To realize the destructive power of political, religious and economic dogma to create suffering is shocking. Even more shocking is this: if we use the definition of dogma as "a set of second-hand beliefs" and honestly examine how much of what we believe is actually second-hand and how much is our first-hand knowledge, we would be dumbfounded. We would recognize that we know very little about reality. We would realize that what we don't know is a whole lot more than what we do know.

So why on earth do we settle for dogma, believing in something that we don't know is true when there is so much of reality out there that we don't know, that we can try to know? We settle for faded fables when the shining truth is just behind the curtain of all the concepts, names and labels we give to things.

To come to these realizations, as demoralizing and deflating to our minds as they are, is an important epiphany on the spiritual path. To see the destruction that dogma has created can break our hearts, but maybe our hearts need to be broken . . . broken open. With these understandings, we can find a renewed desire to let in any experience that comes along in life as it potentiality could contain the seeds of awakening, unlike those caught in dogma who only consider that which confirms a pre-set belief system.

There's a saying that "if you want your life to change, your have to give something up". I'd like to suggest that one of these things we should continually learn to recognize and give up is dogma. The best place to start is inside our heads. It is not only a great service to ourselves, it is the best gift to the world.

> *"We must approach life as though stepping from a dark chamber into a lighted one for the first time, without anticipation or expectation as to what we are to see or hear and then subject each experience to our own analysis, not coloured with the analysis of others. The person who really wishes to approach the mystical life in a frank manner . . . must not be a coward. He must not hesitate to oppose or challenge tradition"*
> Ralph M Lewis. *The Sanctuary of Self.* AMORC

CHAPTER 6

PERSONAL REALITY AND ULTIMATE TRUTH

INSIGHT
Personal Reality

We all have experienced insight before. It is that flash of knowingness that often accompanies the concentrated contemplation of a problem. It can appear out of nowhere, often when one is no longer directly contemplating the problem. It is often accompanied by feelings of relief or delight. It can offer solutions to creative projects, personal dilemmas or business endeavours previously not thought of. These epiphanies can cover the gamut from how to re-arrange the furniture in a room to the solution of complex problems in physics. Insight cannot be forced to happen and although there are processes we can employ to improve the probability it will occur, nothing can guarantee its appearance. As Einstein once said: "The intellect has little to do with the road to discovery. There comes a leap in consciousness, call it intuition or what you will, and the solution comes to you and you don't know where, how or why".

Generally, insight occurs when an intense focus on a problem or question has been followed by a period of letting go of the problem

That is, active concentration is followed by passive receptivity. Edison and Einstein commonly followed this procedure to gain their inspirations. Sometimes insights can occur by contemplating one side of a choice and then the opposite over and over again to produce a solution that is a combination of the two: i.e. thesis, antithesis and synthesis. Another way to facilitate insight is a process of bisociation where two elements or items not normally associated with one another are connected to produce an unexpected third element. This is often the method behind comedy. I once saw a comedian from Newfoundland do the famous "To be or not to be, that is the question" in Newfie jargon. "Ya either is er yer isn't I figrs." Another method is to repeatedly expand and then contract the problem with contrasting full communication and summaries so that previously unclear elements of the problem are revealed and then re-stated until the problem is fully understood. As the solution is often hidden in the problem, a fuller understanding of the problem can often result in a solution insight. (See the exercise on Problem Solving for this technique)

But even with these techniques there still is not a direct link between where we started and where we ended up. There is not a conduit or process that contributes to the insight, as with sensation, or a connection between all the elements in the process like the way logic works. There is no "via" or "by way of". The insight is spontaneous. It is often accompanied by a sense of exhilaration, as the tension between the problem and solution dissolve, or laughter at the obviousness of the solution. A common element of insight is the certainty of its reality or its appropriateness to the situation.

There are many theories about how the phenomenon occurs. One theory is that our inner consciousness is continually mulling over the various permutations of a problem, combing through many combinations of the elements of a situation as we go through our lives. Another idea is that spiritual beings psychically present a solution to us after investigating the entire set of options from a much more expanded viewpoint. Others who are more materialistically-inclined suggest that it is just a neurological event much like a computer sorting through and comparing probabilities and arriving at the best possible solution.

Whatever the explanation, we often do not know how we arrived at the solution. It just appears. We know the idea is right and true even though there may not be logical proof. If asked how we know it is right, we would just say that we know. There is an inherent feeling of validity.

Personal Insight and Spiritual Awakening

It is important, however, to distinguish between personal insight and spiritual experience. Insight is most often related to our personal reality or our personal situation in life. For instance, we may have an important understanding of how our behaviour originated in childhood or how to best use our body to swing a bat to hit a home run. These ideas will be true for us but may not be true for others. The mistake is that we may think that what is personally true for us is also true for others.

Some spiritual teachers make the same error. A guru may think that in his/her tradition, a particular meditation practice is good for everyone at all times when, in fact, other forms of meditation may be more suited to a person's disposition. A more nervous, physically active person may find a walking meditation more beneficial, whereas an introverted person might do better with sitting meditation. We should not make the mistake that our personal preferences, such as the clothes we wear, our habits of communication, our goals in life, or our individual values, should be the preferences of everyone else. We should understand this is just the truth or the way-it-is for us.

But on the other hand we should also know that just because we have a personal reality it does not mean that there is not a universal truth that applies to everyone. This can also be another error on the spiritual path; i.e. believing that there is no such thing as a universal truth. It is easy to assume this, especially after going through the former list of all the ways we are limited in our perception of the truth. Since all the processes that we normally use to try to know the truth can't get us there, we may be tempted to conclude that there is no way we can know the truth, or that there is no universal truth to be known. This is a recipe for cynicism and despair at the possible meaninglessness of life.

The good news is that the truth can be known and there is a way that we can discover the truth for ourselves. This idea, this path, may be new to us. It is a revolutionary path that involves a new form of consciousness. It is called "Direct Experience".

DIRECT EXPERIENCE
The True Nature of Self, Life and Others

This form of consciousness has been called by many names through the ages. A few of these labels are "awakening", "enlightenment", "illumination", "transcendence", "self-realization", "kensho" in Zen, "anubhava" in Hinduism and "unitive consciousness" in modern psychology. It is often described as a life altering spiritual experience where one suddenly breaks through one's normal mode of sensing to become cognizant of the true reality of existence. It is also accompanied by a deep sense of peace, serenity, bliss and inner harmony. Because it results in an exalted awareness of self, it is always life altering.

Direct Experience is often described in terms of what it is not. Like an insight, it is not accessed through a 'via' or a process, such as sensing or logic. It is also not subject to affirmation, visualization, positive thinking or believing. As was illustrated earlier, we can very easily manufacture an exalted sense of self through a process of repeating an affirmation or visualizing a scene of being atone with the universe but this experience will fade without continual reinforcement.

Direct experience differs from insight in that it is much deeper. With insight we are in-sight. We are on the outside of a problem or issue, looking in-side and seeing the essence of the phenomenon. With direct experience, we are in union with the thing we inquire into. We enter into it with our full consciousness. The duality between the perceiver and the perception are gone. For a brief moment in time, we are no longer separated from our real essence. We have merged. We are one with ourselves or with life.

It is often described as a spontaneous event, a profound "aha" moment, a deep intuitive flash that lights up one's being. Suddenly we know who we are but this occurs in a way that is much more enveloping than an insight. It encompasses one's whole body, mind, emotions or one's whole being. With it there is a universal understanding or knowingness of the fact or the Truth of one's existence. We are united with our true nature in such a way where we are not only experiencing the magnificence of who we are, but we know with absolute certainty the fact of our being. Here is an account of an awakening experience:

> *"Suddenly I knew who I was. Tears just streamed down my face, I was so overwhelmed. It was so simple . . . and I was so grateful, not just for what I discovered about myself, but also for the total certainty associated with that experience. There can never be any doubt . . . I knew it in a way that didn't depend on any feeling, idea, belief or anything—I was just directly conscious of who I was."*
> —P.C.—Academic

The Spontaneous Event of Awakening

Awakening does not happen through a process. It defies understanding because it is a paradox. It is a way that has no way. It is an experience that initially is not an experience and then it becomes an experience. It is a knowingness that is beyond thought but we try to feebly describe it through thought.

To be more specific, in direct experience there are three spontaneous events that occur: union, knowingness and experience.

1. **Union:** Our consciousness spontaneously fuses with the essence of our true self, life or another for a timeless instant. Some people describe this union like an implosion: all the separate parts of ourselves become one. The separation between the observer and the observed disappears.

2. **Knowingness:** We become suddenly conscious of that with which we have united. Without any procedure or method for arriving at this understanding, we know the essence of it absolutely. It is a complete understanding, an illumination or an influx of knowledge that transcends and far surpasses that which is ordinarily experienced or communicated by us.

3. **Experience:** As we fall out of the unity, or the implosion, into truth, we now explode into the experience of ourselves, life or another from the new vantage point. There is a new awareness that was not there before. It is similar to going into a darkened room and turning on the light. When the room was dark we could see nothing, but now with the light on we see everything. We have become en-light-ened about the room, becoming conscious of what was always there but we overlooked. For instance, if we have suddenly fallen into the knowledge that we are divine love or everything or pure absolute potential, then we move into the exhilarating experience of that. There is an energy release and our presence begins to radiate almost as if there is a light within us. Some people's experiences can range from the gamut of extreme bliss and joy to a grounded sense of peaceful calmness as they come home to themselves.

However if all of these are not present, the phenomenon is not awakening. We can be deeply in touch with ourselves in deep meditation and feel calm, blissful and serenely at peace but if we cannot articulate who it is who is calm, it is not awakening. Conversely we may be able to intellectually state an idea of self but if we are not in union with ourselves and in an experiential self-connection, it is also not awakening.

Awakening is very much like waking up but waking up in a very unique way. We suddenly become consciously connected to the one that we have always been being (but not conscious of) and the change is noticeable by others. There is an obvious change but we do not change into something else. Actually what happens is that we drop a piece of the personality in which we have been trapped and fall into our true authentic self, becoming more able to present ourselves from this radiant state. What we become is ourselves, not someone else. We become who we have always been being, though not conscious that we have been being. It is simple, exhilarating and revitalizing.

> *"The Ultimate is not something you attain; it is something you merge with. It is something you become."*
> —Sadguru Vasudeva, *Eastern Wisdom*

With awakening comes tremendous benefits: inner peace, self-acceptance, fuller authenticity, inner certainty, the ability to connect deeply with Self and others, enhanced meaning and purpose and a deeper capacity for happiness and joy. Because one's life is based on a solid foundation of immutable truth, there naturally arises a greater strength to face any experience in life and persist through difficult times.

We realize that ultimate Truth is knowable and it is already in us, because in reality we are it. We are the truth itself.

ASPECTS OF DIRECT EXPERIENCE

Obvious Simplicity: Spiritual literature is full of accounts of spiritual seekers having enlightenment experiences and laughing uproariously. It is because Self, life and others are completely obvious and naked, no longer in hiding. They are there for all of us to see. The truth is as obvious as the nose on our face. We don't see it because the mind is so full of ideas, beliefs, prior experiences, and concepts that we project onto our view of reality. It is as if we were wearing rose-coloured glasses and concluding that everything has a red tint. But when we take off the glasses, the world is brand-new. It really isn't any different; we are just seeing clearly for the first time. When we live from this pristine quality of perception, we tend to be more content with the ordinary, realizing that there really is no other place to go in life. Everything we need is here now, even the ultimate truth. The greatest fulfillment is found in the present moment. We welcome being an unpretentious human being.

> *"I yam what I yam, yuk, yuk, yuk, yuk, yuk!"*
>
> —Popeye

Permanence: In order for something to be true it needs to be that way all the time. If it changed then it would not be true. For example true love is not true if at some point the person does not love anymore. True love means: "I'll love you 'til I die". When we realize the truth of Self, we will perceive the God-Self that has always been being us and will continue to be us in spite of the changes in our bodies, personalities, careers and relationships. This realization brings an inner strength and security. We know that no matter what happens to us, we will not be destroyed and we will still exist. The fear of not existing or of dying is behind most of the fears that defeat us in life. With the realization of the immutability of the true Self, we are able to face and overcome life's greatest challenges.

*"Ultimate experience gives ultimate knowledge which casts
out the ultimate fear, the fear of death."*
—Ram Dass

Universality: When we realize the way that life, others and Self actually are, we understand that it is this way for everyone. It is the foundation of all philosophy and religion. After a direct experience we can understand the deeper meaning of spiritual texts and spiritual writings. We understand that the divine dwells in all beings and all things and we have more compassion for our fellow humans. We feel a greater connection to the greater mystery of life and feel at home in it. We feel a greater reverence for the planet we live on and the universe in which we dwell.

Factualness: Direct experience is not dependent on acceptance or non-acceptance. It does not care whether we like it or not. It is not subject to us admiring it. It just is as it is. The truth exists independent of our awareness. Even if we are not aware of it, it is still there. It is not dependent on anything for its existence. No matter how much we affirm it or deny it, or curse it or bless it or proselytize or condemn it, it will still be. There is an inherent authority about it. What is experienced is never detracted by any doubt of its authenticity. There is always an inner conviction. Direct experience does not require reinforcement by faith, belief or affirmation. We always know the divine truth, even though we may fall out of the experience of it.

*"Once one has seen the elephant, it is no longer necessary to
accept on faith that the elephant exists."*
—Early Zen saying (Soto school)

Reality: In fact, truth is the only thing in life that is real. Falsehood does not exist. It has to be invented. And in the face of truth, falsehood doesn't stand a chance because the truth is the only thing that is real. When illusion stares the truth in the eyes it vanishes into the dream from which it arose. So when we experience the actuality of Self and life, our sense of self-rejection lessens. Others' opinions about us matter less. We are who we are and life is what it is, no matter what others or we believe. There is a certainty and unpretentiousness that will enter our lives from this. The tendency to try to be like someone else is lessened as we begin the new task in life of living in our authentic presence, presenting ourselves as we really are. Falsehood requires a lot of effort and forcing to be maintained, made consistent and promoted.

When we experience the actuality of self and life, we experience a release of the life energy that has been required to prop up a false self and when we communicate our new awareness fully to another, this life energy becomes available to move through the body and create greater health and psychological wholeness. Those who have awakened have radiance about them. It is this authenticity that others really want from us in all our relationships. This authenticity is the result of being with reality as it is, even though when we enter into the direct experience it appears as if we have transcended reality or entered a state that is in some way in an outside alternate dimension. In actual fact, we have for a brief period of time broken through the grip of everyday illusion that we have existed in and entered into reality. What we directly experience in awakening is actually normal reality. We have not transcended at all. The whole idea of transcendence is an error.

Ineffability: The awakening experience is difficult to communicate because it is beyond words or concepts or beliefs. Any experience itself, whether direct or indirect, loses something in the explanation. How can we get across the totality of the experience of eating a peach? The sensation of taste cannot fully be converted into words.

The situation is even more problematic with a direct experience. Enlightenment is a shock to the mind. It surprises the ego because it is beyond its domain, beyond its governorship and outside its kingdom. The mind grapples with trying to force it to fit into the landscape it has fashioned but it cannot. Sometimes the mind will try to deny the experience because it does not conform to the picture it has made up of the Self, life or others. If it is successful at this denial, then the experience will become a memory but it is not really gone. It has just been covered up and years later at the right time it will surface in all its glory. Because of this inability of the mind to explain the knowingness, many spiritual traditions advise students to not do anything with the direct experience and avoid communicating it. This is a big mistake. The mind needs to make sense of it, to digest it as it were, to correlate prior experiences and confined concepts with the new experience and in so doing expand past our limited understanding of reality. This is best done by externalizing the experience by communicating it to a receptive other person. Doing so helps to integrate the awakening and bring it into a more embodied form. It is for this reason that authors write and teachers teach, since the act of communicating helps them access more of what they know and solidify their understanding so that it is more livable.

Liberating: Jesus once said: *"Know ye the Truth and the truth shall set you free"*. When we come to know the essence of Self we are released from the imprisonment of an illusion we have believed for many years and dramatized that has caused much suffering. With awakening comes a release of energy that is the result of letting go of the effort that it takes to keep positive and negative beliefs in place. It takes a lot of internal psychic energy to hold onto these beliefs. When we realize the truth, we can let go of the need to hold onto these beliefs, because no amount of believing or disbelieving can change what is. The truth is not dependant on anything for its existence. A dog does not need to affirm that it is a dog in order to be a dog. That effort is not required. But if the dog did not know what it was and thought it was supposed to be a cat, it would need constant energy to maintain resistance to its true nature and the belief in being a cat. I have witnessed many individuals who have carried around significant pain in their lives as the result of a decision that they made about themselves due to an early childhood trauma. When they revisited that decision and realized what the choice was (e.g. that they were not to blame for what happened to them as a child), the years of pain that had tormented them dissolved right before their eyes. I find it absolutely amazing to witness how this happens for others. They become freer to act from the true individual they actually are.

> *"As we awaken we discover that we are not limited by who we think we are. All the stories we tell ourselves—the judgments, the problems, the whole identity of the small self, and the body of fear'—can be released in a moment, and a timeless sense of grace and liberation can open for us."*
> —Jack Kornfield

There is a great power in knowing the truth. We do not have to believe what we already know. We just accept it. We do not have to prop up, justify, defend or proselytize what we know. All that neurotic force is dropped and we come home to a deeper discovery: the true happiness that we have been socialized to believe by our modern media that is supposed to be outside our Self is already within us.

It arises naturally as a result of just being as we are. We do not have to do anything or have anything. Happiness is inherent in our being. The neurotic addiction to finding happiness outside fades and the more we stay in touch with our true nature, true peace of mind arises. We realize that life is fulfilling to the extent that we are being ourselves in whatever experience we are having. There is a permanent sense to the Self and, as result, the fear of experiencing life begins to vanish. We are less distant from life and others and life is lived, deeper more profoundly. Consequently, we have a greater willingness to experience life and process life experiences. The wisdom that is naturally there in our world we can now access.

> *"When you know who you truly are there is an abiding
> alive sense of peace. You could call it joy because that's what
> joy is: vibrantly alive peace. It is the joy of knowing yourself
> as the very life essence before life takes on form. That is the
> joy of Being, of being who you truly are."*
> —Eckhart Tolle

I realize that much of what I have presented here in this chapter is intellectual and I might be subjecting you to the same trap of trying to transmit the essence of a direct experience in words—one of the things I have been warning you about that the intellect cannot do. So I would like to present to you an account of an enlightenment experience that a participant had on an Enlightenment Intensive, one of the retreats I facilitate. Compare this to the enlightenment of one of literature's great figures, Alfred Lord Tennyson. Feel into the experiences and see if you can get a sense of the power and profoundness of the nature of direct experience:

> *"It was as if everything was connected, connected to me.
> All smells, all sounds, all sights, all things sensory seemed
> to be totally happening in me or me in them. There was
> simply no separation between me and light, me and sound,
> me and fragrance, me and other than me. I couldn't tell
> if I was hearing the sound in my head or where the noise
> originated. It was as if the image I saw was both in me, of
> me, as me. Isolation, separation, feeling alone or closed was
> absolutely not the case.*
>
> *I understood in that timeless moment all the teachings
> of the great ones—, Jesus, Gandhi, Martin Luther King,
> Martin Luther King, Lao Tzu. I knew everything. I was
> living in the Tao. I was all things, all time. I was absolutely
> everything and nothing at all in the same moment."*
> —Stephen Garrett, Langley.
> BC—Enlightenment Intensive Participant

> *"All at once, as it were, out of the intensity of the consciousness of individuality, the individuality seemed to dissolve and fade away into boundless being: and this not a confused state, but the clearest of the clearest, the surest of the surest . . . utterly beyond words, where death was an almost laughable impossibility, the loss of personality but the only true life."*
>
> —Alfred Tennyson in
> *Cosmic Consciousness* by Maurice Buck

CHAPTER 7

ENLIFENMENT

AFTER AWAKENING

It's often said: "Before enlightenment chop wood, carry water. After enlightenment chop wood, carry water," and this is true. We go back to our life where all the normal activities of life still remain. As I said at the beginning of the book: *On the outside we look like everybody else. We talk, walk, eat, sleep, work, relax, earn money, pay bills, wake, dream . . .* yet on the inside we are different. After awakening, we are awake to the divinity of life, others and ourselves. We now see others and life from a new and truer vantage point. We have a more intimate relationship with ourselves within all the same endeavours in life that we had before direct experience. We have been to the mountaintop, tasted truth, seen divinity and experienced a more expansive vista of reality. In many ways, it is like a re-birth. There is first our physical birth. We are born into a body but over time, with trauma and socialization, we loose the connection with our True Self. If we are lucky at some time later in life, we are re-born into our spiritual self by awakening to our essential nature.

Many spiritual traditions consider awakening to be the end of the spiritual path, primarily because in most traditions it takes so long, a lifetime or more, to get there! But now there are modern methods that can take us there in a fraction of the time. (*See the chapter on the Enlightenment Intensive*). It's a paradox. Awakening is the end of the path and it isn't. It is in the sense that it is the end of the searching for Self. When we "answer" the question: "Who am I?" that is the end of the project. It's a done deal. We know for certain who we are. To ask the question anymore is fruitless often exasperating. Asking it is as useless as asking "how do I get to the supermarket" when we are already there. But there is more to the spiritual path than just awakening.

"True-Self-Actualization"—*Be-You-to-Fullness*

As the problem of "not knowing the Self" is resolved, a new problem arises: the project of how to live from this awakened state. In some circles this can be called self-actualization, but I prefer to be more specific. The terms: "True-Self Actualization" or "Enlifenment" is more descriptive. It is the process of cultivating and living from our new awareness once self-realization has occurred. In other words, it's not just enough to have an enlightenment experience; we must work towards, what we might call the "Steady Being", the state of being in touch with our True Self and consistently relate to others from our essential nature rather than through our personality or reactivity from past trauma. Enlifenment or True-Self Actualization means to move from Self-realization or an Enlightenment experience to full Enlightenment. Although there are many definitions for someone who is fully enlightened, depending on the spiritual path one is on, it generally refers to someone who has fully dissolved the reactive mind so that they are no longer being stimulated and over—or under-reacting to present circumstances because of past trauma. They are surrendered to life with no tendency to resist or grasp onto pleasant or painful experiences i.e. they respond to life and others appropriately to the situation and they are in constant identity with the universal Self and radiating wisdom, peace and compassion. Let me use a couple of examples:

Cultivating the Awakening Experience

Ramana Maharshi, one of India's greatest sages, while inquiring into the question: "Who am I?" had a profound enlightenment experience at a very young age. It is reported that he spent the next 10-20 years deepening and integrating his self-realization until full enlightenment. It is also reported that after Buddha had his "big bang" enlightenment experience, he spent many months continuing to sit in meditation. What were they doing? My theory is that they spent this time putting their attention on their True Self and letting the Enlightenment grow, mature and ripen. Let me explain it this way. In many ways the possibility of awakening is like a seed that dwells latently within us. Who we actually are is always there but is just not seen. However when we water it, with the spiritual practice we have been doing, at some unpredictable moment that seed will burst open with new life akin to the bursting forth of the new awareness of directly experiencing existence. This is the new life, the new birth that I have talked about, but in order for that seed of awakening to grow, it needs to be further tended with sunlight, watering, nourishment and weeding. How do we do this?

Let's look again at Buddha. My theory is that he stopped the technique he was using to get enlightened because it was no longer necessary. He was now in union with the divine itself and as a result he just resided in it. Another way of saying this is: he focused his attention on his new knowingness as his meditation practice and let go of the technique that got him enlightened. He did not need it anymore. In so doing, his awakening and knowingness continued to expand. There is a universal principle that whatever we put our continued attention on comes more into existence. We have many new-age philosophies from *The Secret* to the *Law of Attraction* that have re-introduced this principle from many age-old mystical traditions. In accordance with this principle, he was putting the (sun) light of his attention on his true Enlightened essence and as a result brought his real Self more into fullness.

So after Enlightenment, we need to spend a good amount of time letting go of the technique that got us enlightened and place our attention on the fruit or the realized truth that we realized in order to ripen and stabilize that experience.

Presenting the Self

In the case of the Buddha, he began communicating what he had experienced to only a few students. As he did this, he became clearer about what he knew. By teaching what he directly experienced, his knowingness became solidly integrated within his being. The more he spoke of what he experienced, the more he understood. The more he understood the more he saw within himself. The more he saw within himself, the more of his True Self he was able to put his attention on. The more he put his attention on his True Self, the more he was able to embody and be in union with it. The more he was in union with it, the more he was able to speak of it. It was a spiraling evolution of his consciousness. So again, following his example, we need to spend time journaling, communicating or teaching the experience to another in order to bring the awakening into greater understanding,

Community

He then created a *sangha,* a community of like-minded people that were searching for the Truth, to align with fellow seekers. They didn't have to hide their aspiration for the Truth. They supported each other through the barriers to Enlightenment thrown-up by the mind and were accepted when authentic awakening occurred rather than being regarded as crazy. Students could seek the truth in the solitary fashion as it was traditionally practiced but they did it together. *They had to do it by themselves but they did not have to do it alone.* Within this community they could cultivate the skill of being in the true essence of themselves, i.e. practicing one's presence and bringing this beingness into the doingness of their lives. (Be-you-to-fullness).

Clearing the Mind and Emotions

I would like to suggest that had psychotherapy existed at the time, the Buddha would also have recommended it for the following reasons. When Enlightenment occurs, even though the knowledge of Truth remains, the high or the exalted state of perceiving our experience fades over time. For instance, if we have been to the Grand Canyon, we have the knowledge of what we saw and we have reveled in the experience. If we look back a few weeks later, the "high" is gone but the memory is still there. Similarly, as time advances after a direct experience, the personality comes back in and we can lose touch with the experience. The knowingness is there but not the experiential connection. However, the personality is not as strong as before. We have had a powerful transformational event of de-identifying from the ego. The neurotic fixation is no longer cohesive and elements of the ego begin to dislodge. This may take the form of surfacing memories, emotions, physical sensations or the trauma, as I described earlier. These can overwhelm us.

> *Enlightenment has then two sides: abiding in true nature and liberation from all rigid and fixed structures. In fact, the more one is liberated from ego structures and their patterning influence, the more one is able to abide in true nature.*
>
> —A.H Almaas, *The Inner Journey Home*

A major error on the spiritual path during these times is to use meditation techniques, such as concentration on the breath, a mantra, the guru, etc. to force the meditator back into a calm state of equanimity to push away the emotional material that has been dislodged hoping that this too shall pass. In actual fact, what some meditators are doing is using their practice to separate themselves from, or suppress, what they are unwilling to experience. The calmness that appears to be there is actually the result of dissociating from the emotional body. It is the result of emotional dullness not emotional clarity. True equanimity is more of a result of clearing the mind of its reactivity, not enforcing emotional passivity which comes from distancing ourselves from the emotions or sensations. When the mind is cleared through effective psychotherapy, then the True Self has fewer impediments to its radiance shining through.

The spiritual path is not about being addicted to calmness or equanimity, it is about responding appropriately to the situation at hand without over—or under-reactivity to resolve the presenting issue. If, for instance I am being attacked, I may need to respond to my attacker physically or run rather than be passively equanimous.

A good short-term block of psychotherapy sessions can be of tremendous help in releasing the hold of the ego and the reactive mind over the True Self so that we can present more of who we really are in our work, family and all other relationships on the path of our true self-actualization.

> *". . . meditation on its own is not particularly effective at solving people's emotional problems. It can prepare the ground, so to speak, by making the person more accepting and less defensive, but without a therapist's intervention, there is very real danger of paralysis."*
>
> —Mark Epstein, PhD,
> *Thoughts without a Thinker*

> *". . . experience and recognition of true nature, regardless on what dimension of subtlety and completeness, do not automatically dissolve all ego structures. Unconscious elements of the psyche are not impacted by conscious experience directly, except maybe in exposing them to consciousness in some occasions. These structures are impacted only by awareness of them and complete understanding of their content. The Enlightenment experience may give the individual a greater detachment and presence that might make it easier for him to confront these structures and issues without being overwhelmed by them, and have a better*

opportunity to work through them. The greater presence
that may result might make it easier for the individual to
abide more in true nature and in this way have greater
detachment from the influence of the structures . . . But the
structure will not self-destruct simply because the soul has
seen the light."
—A.H Almaas, *The Inner Journey Home*

Practicing Presence

Another important practice is the practice of self-remembering or "practicing the presence". This is a simple practice of placing our attention on our True Selves, especially in our interactions with others.

The real difficulty in coming back into life after an Enlightenment Experience is that people will perceive us differently, judge us and want us to conform to how they think we should act or how we used to be. They will see a difference in us but in reality we are not being somebody else. We are actually being more ourselves. We are presenting more of who we are and less of our social personality. So we are paradoxically different but the same. This can be a major challenge after an Enlightenment experience, as we can be tempted to abandon our connection to our True Self in favour of contracting into our limited ego, fearing the judgments or rejection of others.

Being able to shift our point of view to let others have their critical opinions without taking them personally is crucial. As one of my retreat participants said "If I am a phony, it's inevitable that some people will like me and some people won't. If I am real, it's inevitable that some people will like me and some people won't. Since I can't get everybody to love me all the time, I'd rather be liked or disliked for being myself".

There is a saying: "There is a King or Queen in all of us and if we notice it, it will come out." So the more we put our attention on ourselves, especially in the crucible of our relationships with others, the more we will develop our ability to live from our divinity.

This activity of self-remembering takes courage but it will help us bridge the gap between the spiritual and everyday life that many spiritual seekers feel. The ultimate test of the Enlightenment experience is how we can live it in life. When we courageously practice being present we will begin to see that life itself is our workshop and our spiritual path of self-mastery. There is no difference between the spiritual and ordinary life.

It is also important that we adopt and continue an ethical lifestyle and vow to treat others well. All spiritual and religious traditions promote this component. If we do bad things to others in our own estimation, we will feel guilty and, out of this guilt, we will hold ourselves back in life, including being more fully in life.

Physical Health and Fitness

Finally, it is important that we continue our personal growth through physical healing and spiritual practices. The body is said to be the temple of the soul and if we are not fit and healthy, we will have difficulty presenting our authentic being. It is also important to continue our evolution through continuing to do retreats, workshops and a daily meditation practice. Even though we have realized our Self, there is still the project of directly experiencing what others are and what life, love, god, truth, mind and consciousness is.

In summary, after a direct experience, the next phase is Enlifenment, which involves:

1. Being with your True Self in meditation
2. Communication of your direct experience
3. A supportive community of friends
4. Psychotherapy, when required
5. Self-remembering in inter-relationships
6. Physical health and fitness
7. Continued spiritual growth practices

If this process of en-lifen-ment is not undertaken and we remain satisfied with just having had the awakening experience without cultivating it in the ways I have mentioned, there is the real possibility that it can become lost. In addition, a phenomenon called "spiritual depression" can set in. It will be as if we have climbed to the mountaintop and reveled in the exhilaration of the glorious view of human potential and experienced the deep fulfillment possible in life only to come down into the valley with people with their noses to the grindstone, bustling about trying to survive in the never-ending necessities of life . . . the people who are unconscious of what it was like at the mountain peak, living their "normal" lives. Our lives can no longer be "normal" because we now know the divinity in life, others and ourselves. But because we have not cultivated our awakening, there is too much of a discrepancy between the so-called spiritual life and real life. It is too far a gap to bridge and hopelessness and depression could set in.

> *"More often than not the ordinary mystical experience of expanded consciousness comes purely by chance, and since it is unconnected with a discipline for sustaining or enlarging it, it effects little or no transformation of personality or character, eventually fading into a happy memory."*
> —Phillip Kapleau, *Three Pillars of Zen*

CHAPTER 8

TO GURU OR NOT TO GURU?

In our journey together we have come a long way with some new understandings and assumptions in order to determine if we need a guru and how we might progress best on the spiritual path. Let us take a look at what we have arrived at so far:

1. The purpose of the spiritual path is to become conscious of the truth of life, Self and others and to fully live from this basic reality.
2. Truth can only be experienced.
3. Overwhelming experiences (trauma) and socialization can block us from knowing the truth and living from our essential nature.
4. Awakening is the direct experience of the truth of life, Self and others.
5. After awakening is the process of enlifement.

Now, with this new understanding of the spiritual path and the nature of truth and awakening, we can finally tackle the guru question: Do we need a guru to lead us to our own direct experience of Truth, free us from our overwhelming experiences and assist us to live from the fullness of our essential nature? And if we do, then what kind of person would this be?

Let us begin by investigating what a guru is and go on from there.

What is a guru? And do I need one?

Traditionally the word "guru" is used in the Hindu, Buddhist and Sikh traditions to indicate a religious teacher. The word originates in Sanskrit and is formed by the syllables *gu* and *ru*. *Gu* indicates darkness and *ru* indicates destruction. Thus, when translated directly, guru means "dispeller of darkness". So it appears that a guru is a spiritual teacher, someone who can dissolve the "en-dark-enment" or illusion in the mind of the student in order to bring them to the opposite state, or Enlightenment.

The question is: How do they do this? How do they dispel the darkness? How do they free us from our illusions? We need to get an informed answer to this question, since we run the risk of more delusion, or en-dark-enment, if we don't.

Does the guru wave a magic wand to clear the darkness, offer affirmations, hit us on the head, speak to us logically, convince us with scientific evidence that there is no darkness, enlighten us with a special touch or gaze? Or maybe offer us their version of reality? We already have gone over many of the methods that don't bring us to the truth. These don't work so how does a guru do it to us?

Let us consider a statement by a Buddhist monk in the Theravada forest tradition:

> *"The real basis of Buddhism is full knowledge of the truth of reality. If one knows this truth then no teaching is necessary. If one doesn't know, even if he listens to the teaching, he doesn't really hear."*
> —Ajahn Chah, *Taste of Freedom*

He is suggesting that a student cannot be taught to know the truth unless they have already arrived at it. And if they already know it they don't need to be taught. These types of paradoxes are common on the path of enlightenment. What does this mean? How does a guru help a person get to the place where they know and don't need to be taught. There is an enigma here that is unlike anything else in life. In most realms of life people can be presented knowledge and advice that will help them have better relationships, find more satisfying work, be a more effective parent but in the spiritual realm that intellectual understanding does not automatically transmit a divine experience of Self. We are already clear that dogma or second-hand experience doesn't get people to the first-hand experience of awakening. So how does a guru help us if not through dogma?

THE TRUE TEACHER

Once again, at the risk of creating more dogma, I'd like to suggest another assumption to explore . . . that the true guru does not do anything to us but they do something <u>with</u> us. That something is not dogma. It is a technique. The true guru is more like a coach, a mentor or an advisor who teaches us a method and supports and inspires us to experience the divinity within ourselves, for ourselves. It is really not the guru's job to personally dispel the darkness within us. That is our job. If it were up to the guru then, this would only create a dangerous co-dependency whereby we continually need the guru, and without the guru we would be lost. The guru cannot dispel our darkness through intellectual discourse, affirmations, guided visualization, hypnosis, answers, etc. It must be done through something else. That something else is technique.

Now at this point in our exploration I'd like to propose that we change our label for this kind of person to more accurately indicate what we are speaking about. Words are very important here because they orient us in the right direction. I'd like to suggest that we change the term that we use to describe this type of guru to another one: "Spiritual Guide" and spend time exploring a definition that more accurately describes this individual so that for once and for all we have no more dogma gurus.

So let us set out with a new definition. Let us try this one on for size for now; experiment with it and, if necessary, change it later. *The spiritual guide is anyone that teaches us transformation techniques and supports us through the barriers that lead us to enlightenment. The spiritual guide is one who supports us: to release past trauma and illusions, to awaken to the way life is, and the way Self and others actually are and to live from our true presence in life.* The true teacher leads us to the teacher within ourselves.

The Best Spiritual Guides—Techniques not Dogma

In my opinion, the best spiritual guides are the ones that offer us effective techniques and a minimum (or none) of their own beliefs or dogma about ultimate reality. As we have already determined, second-hand belief systems limit us to pre-determined spiritual experiences or get us caught in fabricating experiences that appear to be real but are not. Far superior are spiritual techniques. These could be any method that facilitates our own insight and awakening such as: journaling, art therapy, music, dance, contemplation, group interaction, communication exercises, etc., that are open-ended, devoid of anything designed to bring us to a pre-defined outcome. These modalities should be free of the teacher's belief system and have been proven through years of testing and modification to help the seeker open up to the Truth for themselves.

Training

The spiritual guide should not only offer techniques but training in how to improve our ability and understanding of how to use these. For example, a common new-age aphorism is *Follow your Heart* or *Listen to your intuition.* This is fine to say but it is a recipe for seekers to get confused and lost. How can we follow our intuition if we don't have any training in how to do this? How many times have we heard someone say "my intuition is telling me not to do this", when they are clearly just avoiding and resisting? God didn't tell them not to take advantage of an opportunity that could really help them; it was their fear of change. This is untrained intuition. I have seen far too many people back off from a wonderful opportunity for personal growth when it was presented because their "heart" told them that they should do this another time (and they never do). This is where many self-help books fail. They provide great ideas but not the experiential hands-on training. So true spiritual guides not only offer effective techniques but lead seekers through step-by-step instruction that improves a person's ability to use the method. They offer guidance and support to do the techniques optimally.

The best teachers coach you through the early and on-going barriers as you progress through the various stages to Enlightenment. (You can read about these stages later in the book). They know the pitfalls intimately because they have personally fallen into them and progressed through them. They can teach you how to recognize them and not back away from them. Good spiritual guides can skillfully add their ability to yours to inspire you to face some of these crises and get through them in a balanced way in a fraction of the time that it would take you to do the technique on your own. In addition, the spiritual guide's presence is often an inspiration in itself. The strength of their presence gives us the confidence that we too can awaken in spite of the significant obstacles.

Natural
Although this can sometimes be hard to evaluate, techniques should be natural. They should be based on the way that human beings and life naturally unfold and evolve in consciousness. The best techniques emphasize or focus on these natural dynamics so that they accelerate the process that organically occurs in life. So instead of taking lifetimes for a person to make a breakthrough, it can occur in a matter of a few months, days or hours. A good technique

should allow a balance between seekers following their own unique path to the Truth in their own time, and being encouraged by a facilitator to evolve at a quicker pace. If there is too much forcing by the seeker or the facilitator, it could actually create resistance or a re-traumatization of the individual and actually set the person back in their evolution. Too much forcing can, in some cases, cause purification energy in the body to be released before the person is ready.

For instance, I have heard of a technique of banishing unwanted thoughts. It involves the person thinking a negative thought, then banging their head against a wall 144 times to remove it. This is unnatural. There are breathing techniques that can concentrate too much life energy (or pranayama) in a person's body and cause psychosis. This too is unnatural and forceful.

On the other hand, a common practice in Buddhist meditation of mindfulness is based on gently putting one's attention on the breath to quiet the mind. It is part of the mind's organic tendency to investigate and inquire. So use of this technique is very effective.

The optimal methods should involve a balance between the gradual dissolution of the emotional traumatic material and erroneous mental concepts, and at the same time open us up to the opportunity for divine insight to occur. As this psychological material is cleared, there is less in the way of us recognizing our true nature. When we directly perceive our True Selves, there is new space in our psyche for our essential being to fill. The mind then has less illusion to sort through to digest and integrate the awakening into a new understanding. If our cup of erroneous beliefs is already full, we have no space in which Truth can occupy. Without letting go, there is less opportunity for letting in of truth and the eventual letting out of the radiance of the True Self.

"All the prophets, seers, sages and saviours on the world's history became what they became and consequently had the powers they had through an entirely natural process. They

> *all recognized and came into conscious realization of the*
> *oneness with the Infinite Life"*
>
> —Ralph Waldo Trine,
> *In Tune with the Infinite* (1897

I once encountered an individual who told me that his guru's main method of awakening was to notice when he was having a negative thought and to immediately set this aside and to think of a positive thought to replace it. He appeared to be very apprehensive and almost paranoid of his mind and constantly on the lookout for thoughts he labeled as negative. At the same time, he seemed to have a glow about him but the glow seemed almost manufactured. I warned him of the danger of this technique, suggesting that he was merely labeling and judging certain thoughts as bad and wrong and suppressing them. He disagreed and continued with this practice daily. Years later I met a friend of this man who told me he had been admitted to a mental institution with symptoms of what he labeled demonic possession. This seeker had, in essence, relegated all the so-called negative aspects of himself into a rejected part of his psyche. Over a period of time, this compartmentalized aspect of himself became a persona that he condemned as evil. Eventually the pressure that was built up inside this sub-personality surfaced and created an immense amount of suffering for him. The practice he had been taught was unnatural because it artificially labeled certain natural emotions as unwanted and others as desired.

In addition, the best techniques should not create dependency on some outside mechanism or substance to open us up to direct experience. It is okay for instance to start off using a guided meditation from a teacher or a CD, as long as the program is training us to eventually practice the technique on our own. The same goes for certain hallucinogenic plant medicines and chemicals such as LSD, marijuana and ayahuasca. Individuals can often have very divine experiences on these substances. But because people have not arrived at these experiences by themselves, they can create a dependency or even an addiction to them. These substances can by-pass an individual's normal healthy defenses and coping mechanisms and release reactive and traumatic material in the mind that they may not be ready to deal with this, causing an imbalance in their psyche. Some of these substances over-ride our ability to choose to be open or closed down. Some people end up stuck in being open to negative forces and are unable to close down to them.

Part of any good natural awakening technique involves a process of clearing away the reactive mind in a grounded and balanced manner so that awakening can spontaneously occur in its own time. When it does, integration of the awakening experience can happen in a more balanced way, as the new sense of self is incorporated into those areas of the mind that are clear. Dissolution of the reactive mind prepares the ground for the seed of awakening to be planted and to grow. Mechanisms that are used outside of one's control can leapfrog over the neurosis of the mind into the land of direct experience without the necessary clearing work that needs to be done to allow the new awareness to shine through the new open space in one's being.

It may be hard to judge whether or not a technique is natural. I'd like to suggest that if a technique is drawn from a process already in life then the practice of it will automatically bring us more into life. In addition, since life is primarily lived with others, it will bring us closer to others. Some techniques over time create a schism in life where the spiritual life appears as separate from normal life or seekers begin to feel they are alienated from others. These symptoms indicate a problematic technique. A natural technique will open us up to the growth potential in just living our lives. A natural technique draws us into life in such a way that we are more willing and able to face the challenges in life and the contact with others, rather than run away.

Structure
True guides not only offer techniques and training in how to optimally use them without the hindrance of dogma, but they also provide

structure to support the efficacy of the technique. Structure could consist of a conducive environment, a schedule, agreements that create emotional safety, disciplined practice or an ongoing support group. It is very difficult for individuals to open up and face the deeper aspects of their humanity and the human mind in a chaotic environment. Details like a distraction-free, well-ordered retreat setting, a scheduled routine to keep people on track, agreements of confidentiality and non-evaluation of others, provide a container which enhances a sense of safety, focus and security. Protected by this container, we can then throw ourselves into the disciplined application of what is taught without having to continually handle the usual distracting influences of life. Structure could also relate to a daily or weekly routine of practice, follow-up programs and on-going events that keep an individual progressing incrementally. This steady progress can help stabilize and embody awakening experiences and allow opportunities for further breakthroughs to occur.

Contact

One of the most overlooked aspects of any technique is the teacher, or more accurately the awakened presence of the teacher. Something immeasurable and magical can happen when there is a deep rapport and connection between the student and the spiritual guide. If the guide has awakened and had a number of profound Enlightenment experiences, he/she will be relating to us from their True Self with an awareness of what we actually are. He/she can connect from their True Self to our True Selves. Even though we may not be conscious of our True Essence, they are and they can connect with us on that level. As they see us in our divine essence, that contact stimulates our awareness of ourselves to grow. We might say that they are catalysts of consciousness.

There is a principle of consciousness at play here: whatever a person consistently puts their attention on in life, they get more of. If we see the good in our children, the more likely they will be good. If we see the bad, the more likely they will display that. The same is true with a spiritual guide. As the spiritual guide is aware of us in our divine nature, so to do we become aware of ourselves. This experience often occurs in silence and without anything done. Yet without anything being done, something is done, the activation of a deeper awareness of ourselves.

This contact, when combined with the compassionate presence of the guide, creates trust within the seeker and, out of trust, we begin to feel the safety to allow ourselves to re-connect to our true nature, that essence that we had to hide or suppress in childhood when we learned that it was not okay to be ourselves. In this space where we are being embraced in the gaze of unconditional love, we will allow ourselves to grow. This phenomenon is often called *darshan* in Hindu culture, and in western psychotherapy it is often referred to as the therapeutic use of the therapist's Self. It is this divine contact that can accelerate the process of any technique.

> "*The lesson for psychotherapy is that the therapist may well have as great an impact through her presence as she does through her problem—solving skills . . . this kind of silence is what allows us to repossess those qualities from which we are estranged.*"
> —Mark Epstein, *Thoughts without a Thinker*

QUALITIES OF AN AUTHENTIC SPIRITUAL GUIDE
U-n-I-versal Guides

Whether or not you choose to be supported by a spiritual guide, the following are some essential qualities I suggest this individual should embody. This list has been developed over years of being with spiritual guides, through observation of the many spiritual teachers during my time at the Ecology Retreat Centre in Ontario, and through a survey of people on my mailing list.

1. **Awakened and Non-dogmatic.** Has this person successfully been to where you want to go in your spiritual development? Have they themselves awakened? Do they demonstrate a wisdom that indicates they know the human condition and the nature of existence or is it just book learning? "Successful" does not necessarily mean they are a millionaire as that kind of "success" is in another area of life, but do they at least have a balanced life including having awakened? One of the keys to getting to where you want to go in your self-evolution is to work with someone who has been where you want to go. It means they have achieved what you want to achieve and they know how to get there. Has the guide had deep awakening experiences beyond dogma or only awakened within the particular belief limitations of their lineage-teachings. Enlightenment is often a process of unfolding awakenings over time into deeper depths of union with the ultimate where we open up to divine paradoxes that get resolved as we penetrate the depths of the opposites. We may experience the non-existence of the individual self and then later directly perceive that there is a universal Self beyond the idea of existence or non-existence itself. We may open up to the emptiness of clear consciousness only to find that on a deeper level there exists the fullness of divine love within it. We may suddenly see that the material universe outside us is an illusion and does not exist and then later experience that it does not exist outside ourselves because it is all within us. The best spiritual guide uses techniques that are open-ended, that have no particular specific goal other than to awaken to whatever direct experience is there, not to the direct experience that confirms a religious belief system. As I mentioned earlier, many genuine Enlightenment experiences can be denied because they do not fit the dogma of the teacher or because the teacher did not have these experiences themselves. It is best to be with spiritual guides

who have penetrated these paradoxes. The value is that they are open to any awakenings that may occur to us and are able to recognize them. Their recognition can help draw them out so that we will not lose them.

2. **Experienced and trained.** What kind of training and experience have they had? Have they had extensive training and a lot of experience in the method they are using or have they just taken some weekend course and decided to give a workshop? Have they gone through some kind of apprenticeship or tutorship that included a lot of supervision or are they self-appointed experts? How many retreats over how many years have they given? What are the participants of their retreats like? Are they like the kind of person you would like to be? Are they balanced, kind, compassionate, less reactive, etc. How many of the students have awakened and how long has it taken them to awaken? If the guru has thousands of students and very few have awakened, why would you want to study with them? We should be impressed by the results a guru gets not the long lineage he represents. In any other of realm of life, we would be a good consumer and look at the quality and quantity of someone's service. We should do the same in the spiritual marketplace!

3. **Empowering Human Mastery.** Do they see the spiritual path as part of everyday human life or do they see the human realm as something that needs to be endured and somehow transcended or "ass-ended"? Do they encourage your finding wisdom in your own life or do they focus on attaining some kind of esoteric state removed from normal life? The best spiritual guides see no difference between the spiritual life and ordinary life. They see us all as part of the collective fulfillment of existence. They encourage mastery of the mind, relationships, health, and finances, even though

they may not teach all of these subjects. They lead you to see the divinity here and now rather than somewhere else and some time later. They see the reward in living, in just being more engaged in the here and now, rather than finding fulfillment in some other realm. Do they lead people to find the wisdom and self-understanding within themselves or offer quick-fix answers that keep students dependent on the guru? Are they promoting themselves as a saviour or encouraging others to save themselves? A true spiritual teacher will encourage you to be responsible for your own life even to the point of making you face your own victimhood rather than create a false sense of pity that only keeps you stuck. They inspire and motivate you to find the resources within yourself and your own life rather than create a dependency on them. Do they welcome questions and being challenged on their assumptions and ask their students to make their own decisions?

"A guru can only point the way; he/she/it is NOT the Way. A sign on a highway shows you the direction to your destination; it is not the destination."
—Ron Dankowich, Astrologer, Orangeville ON

4. **Morality.** Do they have a moral code of conduct in how they treat their students? If there are agreements or rules of conduct that they ask their students or retreat participants to observe, do they follow these or consider themselves to be exempt? How do they behave around the opposite sex? Do they relate naturally or invite inappropriate flirting or sexual innuendos? Do they promote any ethical or moral standards to live by?

5. **Coherency.** Are they coherent? Do they demonstrate in their behaviour, relationships and work, the kind of life that

you would want to emulate? Do they walk the talk or just give good advice where the rest of their life is in shambles? Do they follow the guidelines and practices they preach to others?

6. **Humanness.** Are they human? Have they been banged up on the spiritual path and gotten through their difficulties? Have they developed wisdom from their experiences? Often the best guides are the wounded healers; the alcoholics who have recovered, the ones that have gone through physical, sexual and emotional abuse and have healed, the ones who have experienced the deep despair of life and found the light at the end of the tunnel. Do they know what it is like to lose a loved one, or have a relationship break up, to get seriously ill and recover? Do they demonstrate human uniqueness and individuality? If they have experienced a lot of suffering have they healed? Have they done their psychological work? Psychological health indicates that the techniques they have used on themselves are effective. Can they share some of their own mistakes and errors in life and use these as teaching experiences or do they present an aura of perfection? This humanness is an important quality because these kinds of guides have empathy and patience with you on your path. What are their beliefs about emotions? Do they believe in a healthy expression of emotions in a way that trauma can be released and healed or is there a fear of emotions? Do they deny or denigrate the emotional world? If so they may lead us down a dangerous path of suppressing or dissociating from our emotions.

"A good teacher/guru/trainer can be an invaluable resource. They are, however, human beings and it is most useful to see them as such. If I put someone on a pedestal and then they show themselves to have human frailties, it is I who

has pushed them off the pedestal, since I put them there in the first place."

—Jonathan Kramer, Instructor. Dynamind
"The Science of Happiness" Newmarket, ON

7. **Compassionate.** Are they compassionate or critical and judgmental? Are they coming from a place of sincerely wanting to help others out of love and concern or are they self-interested? Unconditional love is important for us to feel safe to enter into the tender areas of hurt and let go of suffering. Compassionate direction from a spiritual guide invites our uniqueness and authenticity to gradually surface through the neurosis of the ego rather than condemn our imperfections with the hope that this will eliminate these characteristics and cause the true individual to emerge. Do they judge you for making mistakes or help you let go of your self-recrimination and guide you to find the lesson in your error?

8. **Humility.** Is there a lack of ego in the teacher or a manufactured charisma? Is there direction to exalt and accept yourself or a sense of them promoting their own adulation? Even in their humbleness, is there a sense of natural radiance, happiness and peace of mind that naturally comes from within or is it somehow pumped up? Are they uniquely themselves or presenting the commonly accepted persona of the "guru" in their speech and actions? Are they accountable? If they make a mistake, are they willing to admit it, apologize and learn from it or do they hide them or even worse blame others or the group for their lack of spiritual advancement

9. **Sense of Humour.** Do they have a sense of humour or is there a stoic rigidity about their demeanor? A sense of

humour is a sure sign of being connected to one's True Self. Those that are enlightened take themselves lightly (because they have less baggage to weigh them down). They can see the ridiculousness of the erroneous attachments and ego mis-identifications that trap us and can help us laugh at it all in a way that brings a sense of spaciousness and a new understanding of our human condition. They exemplify the deeper joy and happiness of being free from the mind and being connected to the aliveness and contentment that inherently resides in the True Self.

"When I think of dogma, I think of rules or beliefs. Sometimes it is subtle and sometimes not so subtle. Several years ago, I believed I had found the path for me and my long drawn out search was over. I loved the meditation technique I had learned, and I experienced such huge shifts in my life that I decided to become a meditation teacher myself. Part of this experience included taking vows to my teacher at the time. I was taught (and it is scary to say, that I also believed it) that having him as a teacher was the one and only way to Enlightenment. In my vows, I surrendered my life to him. He was very charismatic, charming and manipulative. Luckily, after a few years, I left that teacher and that path. I am grateful for this experience. I learned many things—including what I want and what I don't want.

Alarms go off for me when I see these similar traits in a teacher or a teaching. I am not interested in anyone telling me how to live my life; what to wear; what to think or who I can have a relationship with. If a teacher wants control, that is the first sign that there is something wrong. In my opinion, a good teacher is one that encourages you to discover the true teacher within. They do not want control, and are not focused on getting money, power, fame or sex. Also, I'm not looking for a teacher who is full of charisma and can perform on Broadway. I'm looking for someone who is there to serve humanity very humbly . . . someone who comes from a place of authenticity, and who has a solid experience of the Truth.

There are many 'wolves in sheep's clothing' out there, and most of them have similar characteristics that I have mentioned. It is so obvious to me when I see them now."

—Diane Yeo, Meditation Teacher,
"The Happy Monks", London Ontario

CHAPTER 9

THE CONSCIOUS SEEKER

We've come a long way in our investigation and I want to thank you for persisting with me in this journey together. We have looked at what the spiritual path is, what truth is, what blocks us from awakening, how we can and cannot experience the divine and what the true spiritual guide is and isn't.

But there is one glaring thing that is missing in all of this investigation: US!

What is our responsibility in all of this? I'd like to suggest to you that this is where the focus of most of our investigation should be. If we have had bad experiences with gurus, are we victims? How can we be accountable so that we have good experiences?

I believe that the solution for navigating our way through the spiritual marketplace is to learn how to become a conscious seeker. This is not something we can be right away. It is something we need to learn. This type of learning is very much like leaning. Just as we lean on a bicycle until it moves or leans on the side of a sailboat to straighten it up, so too we can lean in the direction of an ability that we want to learn. If we force too much, then we may get too fanatical in the other direction. The term leaning implies being gentle with ourselves by making an effort. But we're not to make so much of an effort that we put all of our attention on the action and miss what we become aware of as we engage in the new learning experience.

Lean Towards Responsibility

It may sound like some fluffy new-age truism to hear this, but the fact is we are all 100% responsible for what happens to us in life. This does not discount the fact that there are people in life who try to hurt or take advantage of others, nor is this a way of using spiritual by-passing to avoid opening our hearts in an uncompassionate way to others by saying "you are responsible" or "it's your karma". Look at leaning in the direction of "I am responsible for what happens to me on the spiritual path" as a way of eventually freeing ourselves from suffering. Even if we cannot take responsibility for the trauma that has been inflicted on us by others or by a guru, we can at the least try to be accountable for the limiting conclusions that we have made up about life, others and our Selves as a result of these events. Even though bad things happen to us in life, we are still the ones who decide how to hold or view these incidents in life. No one reaches inside our heads and turns the choice-making switch onto one of the available options. We are the ones who choose.

I know about this all too well.

My Journey to Self-Responsibility

For many years I suffered from the infidelity of women, from feeling trapped in work that I hated, being scammed financially by others, and being a part of two cults where there were sexual, financial and power dynamic abuses. I felt like I could never get ahead in life. Early on in my spiritual path, all this shadow side of my personality started to rear its ugly head. Memories surfaced of six weeks of physical abuse and abandonment when I was in the hospital as a two-year-old, of physical trauma by a neighborhood boy who abducted me when I was three, of several incidents of sexual abuse when I was seven, and of numerous disappointments involving my alcoholic father. I could not believe that I caused these. "How could I as a young boy cause this?" It was inconceivable that an innocent young boy made this all happen. I got angry at people's glib responses to my story: "Oh you created this!"

But I leaned on this idea—"I am not a victim. I am responsible".

The first thing I asked was one of the most important questions that I have ever asked myself. "As a result of these incidents, what belief did I make up?" I realized that I made up the beliefs: "I am no good", "I am unlovable", "I am alone in life", "I can't get what I want", "My needs are not important", "I am a victim" and others. Even though I was young, I realized that no one made me make these things up, it was the inner consciousness within me that had to make sense of the abuse and try to explain it all. I did this innocently because I didn't know any better.

So I worked through therapy and meditation and the co-evolution process (described in another chapter) and was able to dissolve these beliefs. It was these beliefs that caused the later experiences to occur in my life. Even though I could not see how I attracted the abuse, I saw that I created the future experiences of betrayal and victimization through my beliefs. But I kept leaning on the thought "I am responsible" and over the years, images and memories of past lives surfaced. I recalled one past life as a Nazi officer that explained that the abuse in this life happened because in a past life I inflicted pain on others. I needed to experience the effects of abuse so that I would become more conscious and compassionate of others. I saw that the man who had an affair with the woman I loved, who tried to secretly destroy my business and almost drove me to suicide, was a man whom I had deceived and killed in a past life. We had been getting even with one another for many lifetimes. But getting even only made us odd.

I was able to forgive these people and myself and let go of these recurring patterns. In the process I continued my spiritual search and had numerous Enlightenment experiences that gave me the deep knowingness that throughout all the abuse that had happened to me, the essential me had always been untouched. Nothing could destroy who I was. My true nature was still pristine, pure and unsullied. In a very practical way, these deep awakenings allowed me to heal. So the understandings that have liberated me do not come from some superficial new-age theory. They come from blood and guts on the path, as well as relentless investigation.

As with everything else I am presenting, I suggest that you lean on the idea that we are responsible for everything that happens to us on the spiritual path. We need to be accountable for the decisions and actions we take or avoid taking. We need to be wary on the spiritual path and not blindly trust someone because they have a white beard and saffron robe. We don't know what is "arising" underneath that robe or behind the backdrop. We need to remember that if someone is in a body, they have stuff to work out. They are not perfect yet. Trust needs to be earned.

2. Lean towards being your own guru.
Lean on the idea that the ultimate spiritual guide is inside—that is, you. Even though you might be exploring the path of Buddhism or Christianity, we are not inherently Buddhist or Christian. You are always you. We are always the True Self. Our identity is not the religion. We are just putting on the personality of the "ism" or "ity". To put on a label is to get trapped in that label. Ultimately each one of us is the Truth itself. How could we recognize something is true unless it was already in us? There has to be an inner reference point from which to compare it. Each one of us is that reference point because each one of us is the Truth. Hold the idea that the only reason something occurs as being true is because it is the inner guru (Gee You Are You) that is verifying it. It is the existent Truth within us that is comparing what is said by the teacher on the outside with the teacher within. Don't accept this because I say it. Lean on it and one day if you are graced by divine experience it will appear as a reality and free you.

Lean on the idea that the true spiritual path is your life. There is so much wisdom in our lives already; it is so obvious that we miss it. If we can take this point of view, then even if we are on a specific spiritual path, then we can open up to the greater inspiration that may not be part of the tradition we are trying out for awhile. Restricting our unfoldment to only the tradition we are exploring can lead to the viewpoint that "there's no spiritual growth in everyday life". In fact, life is the testing ground. If we want to find out how centered we are in equanimity there's no greater test than facing someone yelling at us when we innocently cut them off in traffic or being with our daughter having a temper tantrum in a public place. There is great learning in life. Lean on the idea that there is nowhere else to go. This is It! *Life is our spiritual path.* And since our life is the ultimate spiritual path we should continually be looking for the wisdom we have found in it. "What did I become aware of today?" "How did I grow in greater ability to be and present my True Self today?" are wonderful questions with which to end the day.

But even though we are ultimately our own guru in the spiritual path of our lives, we should paradoxically be a good student. This means acquiring as much understanding of the philosophy and as much training in the techniques presented as possible. We should be passionate about our learning, asking questions and not going on to more learning unless we have fully understood what has come before. Maybe you will be drawn to become a spiritual teacher yourself. The best teachers have always been the best students.

> *"Like the bee, gathering honey from different flowers, the*
> *wise man accepts the essence of different scriptures and sees*
> *only the good in all religions."*
> —Srimad Nhagavatum—Hindu spiritual text

3. Lean towards your Dogma Detector

We should learn to recognize when dogma is present so that we can decide whether or not we want accept it or not. Here are some recommendations.

The first thing we need is to get clear for ourselves is what dogma actually is. Right from the beginning we should not accept anyone else's definition of dogma even the one that I offer. I will offer my own definition but it is best if we each develop our own. From this deeper insight, we will have an understanding of the features of dogma from which to recognize it. If it is perceived, then we can consciously decide to reject, accept or suspend it. (A way to develop your own definition is to do the co-evolution exercises on dogma in the back of the book) But for the sake of exploration right now, I will offer my own definition of dogma: *a set of fixed second-hand beliefs that we ourselves (or the person communicating them) have not experienced as being true.*

There is intractableness about dogma that indicates: "This is the way it is and there's no other way". There is no alternative view. There is no room for debate or discussion. There is an illusory certainty about it as the person delivers it. One might ask, "Is there not certainty when one directly experiences the nature of one's True Self. What is the difference then?" Yes there is certainty but this comes from union with the Truth. It comes directly from one's Self. There is an inner authority. With dogma the surety is propped up by an external standard. The person who uses dogma is hiding his/her own uncertainty with the vicarious certainty of their teacher or their "sacred" scripture almost like the wimp talking tough hiding behind his big giant friend. As a friend of mine once said: *"She's got it all together. She's like concrete . . . all mixed up and permanently set."*

To detect dogma, the question to ask is: "Is there evidence of rigidity here that is reinforced by an external authority?" As you do this you will be able to identify when dogma is present and then to accept it, reject it or put it on the shelf for further consideration. Here are some specific examples of rigidity:

- **Rigidity of belief:** Notice what the person, system or religion uses to validate their beliefs. As stated above if, they use an external authority (their great Saint says it is true) or they appeal to the number of years of their tradition (it's been around for 1,000 years) or they refer to the rule of the written word (the sacred scripture says it is true), we can assume it is dogma. Often people will say a belief is true because they have faith in it and no amount of argument or presentation of an alternative view can dislodge them. The argument is circular: "My faith has made it true and I believe my faith is true." Often people will say they have experienced a belief system to be true when in fact they only "experienced" an intellectual understanding of it. It makes sense to them. It is the same "party-line" reproduction of reality that is propounded by their scripture, therapeutic system or teacher. There is "hole-lessness" to the holy party-line in which any variation or lack of coherence to the philosophy is explained. There is no aspect of existence that cannot fit into the religious container in spite of the fact that it is leaking all over the place. There is nothing that is unknown and therefore the wonderful mystery of you and me together in the universe is dry and dead. All wonder is gone. Any opposition to the dogma is met with over-reactive righteous indignation or the admonition that non-believers are less advanced spiritually. It is all part of the socialization structure that ensures conformity and is a sure indication of dogma.

"True Religion is sensitivity to reality"
—J. Krishnamurti

- **Rigidity of language:** Are there terms that are used over and over again in spiritual discourse (e.g. non-self, ego, karma, non-duality, Holy Ghost, sin) to explain spiritual phenomena

89

but little originality in the use of this terminology. Certain concepts ebb and flow in and out of "new-age" and religious culture. They come into vogue-like fashion statements and people present them out of a manufactured spiritual personality but the foundation of it all is jargon. Remember that words are very powerful and certain terminology used over and over again can, over time, create indoctrination into dogma. As we know, names are labels and can limit our experiences to certain belief prescriptions and exclude others. Notice if there are common words used over and over again. If so, this indicates dogma. However, if there is other terminology employed that creatively expands these concepts or introduces subtler spiritual understandings or a unique iteration, we can conclude that there is a genuine spiritual experience being communicated. Even so, taking on the unique terminology of others even if it originates from that individual's own direct perception is just creating dogma within us. We should take the time to develop our own personal insights and direct experiences and be wary of limiting our own concepts of Self and consciousness to jargon.

- **Rigidity of attire:** Strict adherence to a particular dress code often indicates adherence to a set of beliefs. This is certainly obvious with established religions where a dress code indicates a respect and an honouring of the tradition but at the same time fosters conformity to that tradition. But certain styles of clothing or common dress (e.g. white shirt and tie) can also serve to socialize followers into a dogma. There may be different attire for the leader that denotes a certain level of spiritual attainment that may not have anything to do with their level of consciousness.

    When I owned a retreat centre I recall serving a group who set-up our meeting hall as a holy temple. I was asked to put a hat on my head before I went into the hall as a gesture of respect for their guru and tradition. A month later, a different spiritual group came to the centre and set-up their meditation hall. I was asked by the monk to take off my hat before I entered the space. I imagined the potential discord if these two groups ever shared the same meeting hall, each arguing over whose hat or lack of hat was more sacred, missing the whole point that it is not the sacred objects that make us holy, it is really us imbuing the object with our own reverence that makes it holy. This act of respect is essentially a reminder to create in our hearts the necessary attitude to establish a sacred container for the worship and spiritual practice that occurs in that space.

- **Rigidity of emotion.** Those stuck in a dogma may have a limited or even a low emotional response. Emotional dullness is often equated with calmness. Spontaneity or a fuller expression of emotions may be held back with the belief that emotional expression, even laughter, is wrong. Excessive seriousness can be evidence of dogma. Those who adhere to a dogma can be more in their minds than their hearts and can use their beliefs as a way to avoid a compassionate response. They can even use the dogma as an excuse to mistreat others. Spiritual by-passing or using spiritual concepts as a way of dismissing the suffering of others or avoiding to take responsibility is common with dogma. "Well that's her karma", "If it is God's will, it will happen", "He created this himself". People stuck in dogma tend to default to these empty aphorisms when they lack the courage to venture into the unknown world of just being with another in their suffering and experiencing that intimate moment where we truly touch another on a soul level.

- **Rigidity of hierarchical structure:** Is there a hierarchy of passing down a belief system, (e.g. Pope to bishop to priest) or a generational hierarchy from one generation to the next. There will always be some variety of indoctrination into a system of dogma in a hierarchy. Wherever there is a structured bureaucracy, belief has to be encapsulated in order for it to be transferred from one generation to the next and dispute is less tolerated. Often the reason there are schisms in religion is because someone in the system has had a deep insight or divine experience that does not fit the prescribed belief construct and they have to leave to avoid persecution.

"The dogmas of the quiet past are inadequate to the stormy present."

—Abraham Lincoln.

I'd like to suggest that even if many ancient hierarchical traditions carry dogma within their teachings, we should not automatically dismiss them. This would be like throwing the baby out with the bath water. Part of the reason that a tradition may have existed for so long is that there is an actual basis of ultimate truth and a genuine foundation of effective techniques for awakening. There is a great value in studying these traditions and their age-old literature and being guided by a teacher for a period of time. Before one has had awakening experiences, one can use these teachings to point the way as long as one is able to identify the dogma. Another value in studying these traditions is being able to recognize in these teachings the description of Enlightenment experiences similar to our own after we have awakened. This can discount the doubt in the mind about our own enlightenment experiences and validate the awakenings.

Just because a tradition is dogmatic, does not necessarily mean we should reject the teachings (just as we should not accept them).

The teachings may in fact be an accurate description of reality; we just don't know they are true because we have not had our own direct experience of them.

This task of "dogma-detecting" is a necessary skill on the path of the "Conscious Seeker". It is no easy task and it is not for the faint-hearted. It requires the courage of a rebel and a renegade, not in the sense of facing an outward tyrant but in facing our inner victim, the one who so easily accepts the theoretical hearsay of others rather than be with our own reality.

> *"We must approach life as though stepping from a dark chamber into a lighted one for the first time, without anticipation or expectation as to what we are to see or hear and then subject each experience to our own analysis, not coloured with the analysis of others. The person who really wishes to approach the mystical life in a frank manner . . . must not be a coward. He must not hesitate to oppose or challenge tradition."*
> —Ralph M Lewis. The Sanctuary of Self. AMORC

4. Lean towards the unknown

This is one of the hardest things to do on the path of transformation: being willing to hangout in not knowing. In our culture there is a lot of investment in being certain. We need to do business with people that know their profession and understand what they are doing. We want to work with people that can give us predictable results. We have been educated to be an expert in a certain field, to be proficient and clear about what we know and what we do. Our employability depends on it. Knowledge is power. Knowledge is money.

But in the realm of awakening, knowledge is actually an impediment. It is a barrier. If we are to find the truth we must go beyond what our present knowledge is. We must go beyond the boundaries of what we know, because we do not know what we don't know. We also don't know what we need to know. And to know the truth we must give up what we now know so that we have a fresh openness for any new deeper insights. We must give up the barrier of the old to find the new. When we hang onto our old knowledge, when we set out into the unknown, the mind just manipulates the new knowledge to fit in with the old. It will overlay the old understanding on the new experience and interpret the present experience with the eyes of the past.

To find the Truth for ourselves, we do not have to say that we are wrong or stupid or deluded about what we know, we just have to set our concepts of reality aside for the time that we are investigating. Instead of being afraid of the unknown, let ourselves replace the fear with an openness and curiosity, as if we are seeing through the eyes of a child. We should approach our search for truth with a sense of wonder and fascination. "Wow, this is a new experience. One that is similar to another experience but totally unique and new. What is this all about?" like a scientist observing an experiment with intense interest. To do this requires an extraordinary sensitivity to take in all the nuances in our inner and outer perceptive field. It requires a new skill of receptivity of moving with and adapting to every shade and colour of reality. And as we do this we will find that heaviness of old knowledge falls away and we move into a new lightness of being. A new deeper sense of satisfaction arises in us as we enter into a new world of wonder with a heightened sense of openness and curiosity. It will be as if we have found a new life, a new evanescent vitality where there is a deep satisfaction that comes inherently out of the natural desire to inquire into our true nature. In reality, this activity of mindfully observing and taking in experience is what all of life is doing anyway: being alive and wanting to know all there is to know of its existence.

"Your time is limited, so don't waste it living someone else's life. Don't be trapped by dogma—which is living with the results of other people's thinking. Don't let the noise of other's opinions drown out your own inner voice . . . and

most important, have the courage to follow your heart and intuition. They somehow already know what you truly want to become. Everything else is secondary."

—Steve Jobs

As we develop this skill of being with things as they are, we will see the tyranny of dogma . . . how dogma makes us dull, contained and replaces our aliveness with something deflated and dead. We will see how those who settle for dogma settle for a reasonable facsimile of life in an effort to avoid the fear of the unknown, even though when on the other side of the veil of the unknown is a world of experience, full of the delight of continual newness. And once we have tasted this new spiritual manna, we can never settle for dogma food again. There's no comparison. Just living life in this new openness becomes inherently fulfilling. Existence becomes its own reward.

We should cultivate being okay in the zone of the unknown. Let ourselves know that we don't know. Be okay with this. It does not mean we are dolts, it means we are explorers. We should try to detect any belief or point of view about reality that we have not experienced as being valid and ask "How do I know this to be true". "Do I know past lives exist? Angels? Karma? Akashic records? Chakras?", "Is there a non-Self or an Atman (Supreme Self)", "Is there a God?" We should not accept anything until we have had the experience ourselves. One of us could be the only person in history that proves all other sages wrong or maybe directly experiences an aspect of reality or a different view of Truth that no one has ever seen before (and start a new movement). After all, this is what Buddha did.

We should avoid rejecting or accepting any belief but rather take it on as an assumption, that it may or may not be true. Let it be tentative. We could look on it as a possibility, like everything in this book, being skeptical but not to the extent of being cynical and rejecting, holding up every point of view about reality that comes our way for later inspection. When we take it in without examination, there is little chance of the growth of a new insight and self-awareness, little growth of real intelligence. It's the lazy way. It's the way of cheating in the school of life by writing down somebody else's answers in the mind.

When we suspend the dogma, we then increase our potential for more insight to occur in our lives. We have more material for our future experience to connect to and to integrate. The more material we have to connect to, the more we integrate the new insight and the more solid our new awareness is. (As in the phenomenon of bi-sociation we explored in the personal insight section).

Many of us have had epiphanies where we have exclaimed, "Ah, yes! Now I understand. That explains it all. This now explains that, explains that, and explains that. I thought I knew it all but now I really understand it!" It's an event where a new insight or even a direct experience connects to a lot of other suspended thoughts and feelings and then it all powerfully comes together. So dogma is valuable insofar as we neither accept nor reject it, but rather hold it out until our own insight allows us to understand it with new awareness.

Secondly, when we communicate our new awareness, we should try to develop as much as possible our own language for our experiences. We can default into the terminology of many ancient traditions, but there is a great value to developing our own language. As we explored in a previous chapter about the importance of our presentation, the very struggle of accessing the right words to communicate our inner realms (even though the wording is still a description, not the real phenomenon) is a way of drawing out that experience and integrating it. It helps us embody or live from our Self-realization. Ultimately, our unique explication is the very gift that the world needs to expand our collective evolution. It is a factor in the co-evolution concept that we will explore in a later chapter.

> "*Mind speaking truth through the lips, or thinking truth consciously can bring all the satisfaction to the world which the world is seeking. Nothing material can strengthen*

people, but the omnipresent can strengthen them with all
the power of truth."
—Emma Curtis Hopkins, Scientific
Christian Mental Practice

Our biggest challenge on the spiritual path is to continually monitor whether or not we are taking on as true, beliefs, points of view, ideas, or concepts that we have not experienced ourselves. We need to vigilantly discriminate clearly between knowledge or understanding and "knowingness"—namely, that which we actually know through our own experience. This practice will be rewarded, eventually with profound insights and inspirations that spontaneously come out of "know" where. Once we have a taste of this divine experience, there will be no going back. We will see dogma for what it really is—a ghost hiding in the shadows trying to convince us it is the light, when we now know the sun shines within us. It will be our own brightness that will be our gift to the world.

"The truth of Illumination is found through honouring
every person's right to have personal truths, following the
voice of his or her own Spiritual essence . . . ignoring the
rigid human rules that evolve when one human wants
others to follow the leader instead of the voice inside."
—Jamie Sams—*Thirteen Original Clan Mothers*

Finally there is one more thing we need to consider to be a conscious seeker. It is probably one of the most important:

5. Lean Towards Personal Psychological Work
Many years ago, when I was the owner of the Ecology Retreat Centre business near Orangeville, Ontario, I was asked to deliver a bowl of fruit to the cabin of one of the spiritual teachers who was running a 2-week meditation retreat. He was a Buddhist monk from the Theravada forest tradition.

I was going through a bit of a spiritual anarchist phase at the time and when I knocked on his cabin door and he opened it, I said irreverently: "Here's your fruit, sir, and do I have to bow down to you before I give it to you?". He laughed and we were instant friends! I had recognized one of his challenges as a guru. He asked me to come in and we had the most wonderful conversation about the conflict he was having in honouring his tradition by wearing his robes. He confided that the robes engendered an idealized fantasy in students' minds of a perfect, realized teacher that he had to frequently dispel by reminding them that he was human, too! (I think he even farted when I was talking to him).

My Human Meeting with an Exalted Man

About 30 years before, I had a similar human experience with the Dalai Lama before he became famous. He had just escaped from Tibet and came to Canada for his first tour. He gave a talk in the Tibetan language in a small meeting hall in downtown Toronto. His interpreter was very bad and we hardly understood a word he said. After the talk, his entourage was clearing a small path in the crowd so that he could exit. During the commotion, somehow I got pushed right in front of him. I did not know what to do, and in shy embarrassment, I automatically put out my hand and said "Hello". There was hush in the audience as if some sacrilege was about to happen. A mortal was going to touch this ideal holy man. Suddenly the Dalai Lama stretched out his hand to me, shook my hand and bowed to me and laughed uproariously. Everyone in the crowd laughed along for about two minutes. It was the most wonderful lesson to everyone: to treat the most holy man as if he is human and to treat the most human person as if he were holy! In spite of the fact that no one understood his talk, that small gesture to me has been the most enduring message of this man's life.

Yet so many spiritual teachers and students get caught in the trap of idolization. Why? Teachers may create that image and juice us with their charisma but ultimately we go along with it. If we put a guru on a pedestal and they topple off and we get hurt, who's to blame? Remember: I suggested that we are all 100% responsible.

There are two further issues that I'd like to suggest you consider. The first is the reality that many spiritual teachers have awakened to the state of unified existence to varying degrees, and we feel the radiance of their clarity, serenity, joy and love. We are drawn to them because the connection to their true essence is causing us to get in touch with our own essence. We are unconsciously resonating to the vibration of their conscious connection to themselves. We are attracted to what they are aware of in themselves, because it is in us, but we are not noticing yet that it is. They are reflecting back to us what we are. We can get enthralled by this and if we are not careful we can only see their divine presence and ignore the fact that they are human beings with frailties, neurotic tendencies and human desires. We may believe that they are flawless. Maybe we forget to notice that they burp, go to the bathroom and think about sex like the rest of us. We may ignore our intuition that something in the way they act is not quite right. We may believe that their dogma is the truth and deny our own experience. It is these human factors that can hurt us just like any other human can hurt us. Yes, we should honour and respect the wisdom they present to us but we must also honour and respect ourselves because, on the level of ultimate Truth, there is no higher or lower. There is no hierarchy. There is only the one Truth that is the same for everyone to experience whether it is you, Buddha, Jesus or me.

The second is that we may get caught in the trap of idolizing a teacher because we have not done our inner psychological work. Maybe we see in the teacher the ideal parent we never had. We may have desperately wanted to experience the unconditional love we missed as a child so that we could grow into the person we could have grown into but if we haven't done our personal work to let go of our early trauma, we will still be unconsciously acting as children. We may attract a guru who we let violate our boundaries in all kinds of unscrupulous and abusive ways just to get that love.

Then we repeat the same victimization that we experienced in our childhood with our parent(s). When the guru falls off the pedestal onto us, it is a nasty way to begin personal work. The student can be re-traumatized to the point where they are hurt for the rest of their life and they may never, ever recover.

We should also realize that being in a relationship with a teacher by accepting his/her beliefs, without investigating their veracity, is essentially an immature relationship. It lets both the teacher, and us, off the hook. We don't have to do the work to find out the truth on our own and the teacher doesn't have to do the work to lead us to our own experience of the truth. It takes effort to be liberated. Freedom is not free. It requires persistence, patience and focused effort.

It also takes a lot of effort, discipline and compassion on the part of a true spiritual guide to let go of teaching dogma and support the seeker to Self-realization. They have to deal with individuals in a journey of purification. They enter into the world of the reactivity of the human mind. The true teacher often holds up a lighted mirror to the seeker who will resist seeing the shadows in themselves and instead project their neurotic patterns onto the spiritual guide. They are tested to stay connected to their true presence in the face of this abnormality. The real teacher knows that the craziness of the human mind is very compelling, yet sees the divinity in all of us. Out of compassion for our suffering, the real teacher jumps into the cesspool. But guides also have to do their own personal work.

Most people on the spiritual path are attracted to the light of the fire on the path but they don't want to face the heat. The deep psychological work of trauma and core belief clearing is essential for us to become whole. This work will help us re-claim what we have neurotically tried to find in the guru: the rejected parts of ourselves and our self-love. It will open the space for more expansive awakening and self-integration to occur and help us for us avoid attracting these types of dogma gurus. We need to walk the journey of awakening as an adult not as a co-dependent child.

"It takes courage to grow up and be who you really are."
—E.E. Cummings

In summary, here are the suggestions on becoming a conscious seeker:

1. Be 100% responsible for what happens on the spiritual path.
2. Be your own guru and take on life as your spiritual path.
3. Be really clear on your personal definition of dogma (second-hand knowledge) and learn to recognize it.
4. Be willing to ask this important question with any new spiritual concepts to which you are exposed: "Do I really know this to be true in my own experience?" and suspend what you do not know to be true and hang out in the unknown.
5. Do your psychological work.

As we approach the end of this chapter, I hope you understand that I am not recommending that you do not have a teacher. That is your decision. I personally have found some teachers incredibly valuable and conversely found others damaging. You may find, as I have, that teachers are very important at some point on the path for a short while or a long while and at some point are not. But let us discriminate between dogma-gurus and spiritual guides and let us be responsible for how we interact with them. Let us be wary of how we create a relationship with them out of our own unmet childhood needs. The same rule in the consumer marketplace applies in the spiritual marketplace: Buyer beware.

We have investigated many of the illusions and traps on the spiritual path and come to some new understandings. I hope, as I have mentioned several times, that you (with the assistance of the exercises at the end of this book) arrive at your own insights. I am not interested in becoming another dogma dispenser. I am more interested in exposing the assumptions and beliefs that keep us trapped so that we can look at these clearly and avoid them. With this in mind, I'd like to expose one more assumption, one that has consistently held us hostage in a big way and use this as a segue into the next chapter.

IS THERE AN ALTERNATIVE TO THE DOGMA GURU?

Over the centuries of spiritual seeking there has been a relatively unexamined curious assumption: there is no alternative to the guru/student relationship. It has always appeared to be the only way to Truth. Trying to go at it alone has been too hard. Many of us, as serious seekers, have assumed that the only way we can get to the door of awakening on the spiritual journey is to follow a guru, and that part of the trade-off is to put up with the dogma. We take for granted that it comes with the package of the guru. Perhaps even the guru has forgotten this.

We have felt there has been no choice. Just like someone who is desperately thirsty will drink polluted water just to quench his thirst, knowing the water may hurt him, so too have we ignored teachings that are tainted with dogma just so we can get the instruction and guidance of the teacher. But is this true? Do we need to get in bed and go all the way with a guru or part of the way or none of the way? Is there another option?

I am here to tell you that yes we may need spiritual guides to teach us techniques to one degree or another, but there is and always has been an alternative. It has always been with us. It can lessen our dependence on a guru and allow us to be more self-reliant.

The existence of this alternative is so obvious it is shocking. When you see it, you will hit your head like Homer Simpson saying "Duh!" When I saw it for the first time, I did the same. I almost put a bruise on my forehead. I was excited about this discovery because, just like you, I'd put up with dogma for years and years thinking there was no other way. Now I am passionate about the alternative. It is why I am writing this book to reveal it to you. In my estimation, it is one of the most overlooked aspects on the spiritual journey. And when you realize it, it will give you some inspiration, excitement and greater freedom to choose to have a guru or to just find the teacher in yourself or at any time to choose both. This alternative is called Co-evolution. It hangs-out in the place you'd least expect it to be: YOUR LIFE.

CHAPTER 10

CO-EVOLUTION

Co-evolution means things evolving together in relationship with one another. Co-evolution is not something new; in fact it is the fundamental basis of reality. It is a natural principle of life that is occurring whether we are aware of it or not. Once we become aware of it, we see it is obvious, in an infinite variety of manifestations.

Darwin was one of the first to notice this dynamic although he described it in terms of physical evolution. He observed that plants and animals adapted and changed according to the influences exerted on them by something in the environment outside themselves. The change that occurred was always with respect to being in relationship to something else. For example, the chameleon developed the ability to camouflage itself as the result of predation from other animals. The bat developed its method of sonar detection in order to locate the insect prey that began coming out at night to mate and feed. Flowers developed interdependency with bees whereby they provided food (nectar) for the bees and the bees in return spread their pollen. This interrelationship through which all things adapt, develop and grow is everywhere in life. Nothing develops in isolation and conversely the reverse is also true, anything that is left in isolation will not evolve and eventually die. So in a physical universe, co-evolution exists.

But does Co-evolution exist on a metaphysical level? Can it be the basis of reality? Is it connected somehow to the growth of consciousness? What is it in our existence that causes us to want to know the truth of ourselves to facilitate self-realization? For the next while, let us take a look at this phenomenon. It's called life.

Let us explore this with a simple imagination exercise.

ALONE IN THE U-N-I-VERSE

Take away everything outside of you in the universe. Take away the planet. Take away the sun and the stars. Take away others. Take away even your body. If there were just a non-physical you and nothing else, how would that be? If you were born that way prior to the existence of anything, into a world with nothing to interact with and nothing to experience, what would be missing?

I'd like to suggest there would be no knowledge of anything in your mind because there would be nothing to experience and probably no thought, because there would be no experience to think about. (As we examined in an earlier chapter, knowledge and thought are the result of experience, and because there would be no experience for the mind to organize, knowledge would not exist.) You would just have pure consciousness empty of content. All there would be would be you, empty awareness and no way of experiencing your Self.

How would that feel? Imagine. It would probably be very lonely . . . maybe even intensely lonely. You would probably have no sense that you even existed. You might even wonder if you were in a dream or a figment of someone else's imagination. You would probably want to know if you existed or not, right? Maybe there would be an urge to find out who you are or to know yourself . . . to gain some self-knowledge?

So what would you want to do in that state?

You would probably want to interact with something outside yourself, to give you some sense of yourself, to have a real experience, at the least.

Now add in the physical universe, including your body, but without people. Imagine you are now interacting with the sky, trees, the soil and the entire natural world. Because you would now be experiencing, knowledge would now start to form. You would learn about food you could or could not eat, animals that were safe or dangerous, the best way to survive, etc. You would develop knowledge about ways to improve your life. You would have to adapt to that world by interacting with it. You would learn about the world by the mistakes and the successes you make. Your adaptation would be the result of your knowledge of the world and resultant conclusions about ways of being and actions you could or could not take. You would be developing not only knowledge about the physical world but some self-knowledge. You would start to understand what you are capable of and the future potential that you have.

But would the loneliness still be there? It probably would. You would still be all by yourself still wondering if you exist . . . wondering who you are. You would probably make the conclusion: "The only way I am going to know that I exist is if something outside of myself similar to me and just as real as me could interact with me and verify my existence. It wouldn't work for me to just interact with trees or chickens or apes because if I did I might conclude I'm a tree, chicken or an ape. I need something very similar to me". That would be a great revelation. You would want other humans in life.

So go ahead and add in other people into the world. Now the real drama begins.

The interactions would go up maybe 1,000-fold along with your experiencing. Imagine how much you would learn about your Self that you didn't know before. Knowing very little about others, you might innocently mistreat others. You might have very pleasant experiences. They might love you or mistreat you. You would learn that you can be hurt and what it is that hurts you i.e. abandonment, lying, abuse, neglect, judgment, cheating, manipulation, etc. You would learn that you wanted to be loved and to love others. You would learn that you wanted to be treated respectfully and to treat others well. You would experience what it was like to be understood and not understood. You would have to look inside for the self-knowledge of how you want to be treated and learn how to communicate to get others to become aware of what you want. You would have to acquire a clearer knowledge of your Self to relate to this.

You would develop an affinity with others that shared similar self-knowledge as you. You would form relationships. In the deep care and bond that others would have for you, you would learn that you exist. You would want others to treat you just as real as they are . . . not as an object but as someone with a similar internal human world as yours, with the same cares and concerns. You would experience wonderful joys and intense suffering. You would innocently take on the mistaken ideas that parents, friends or our culture have about you because you wanted to be accepted and loved as a result. You would probably lose a sense of yourself, form an ego and someday learn that self-love and self-acceptance is more important than others' opinions of you. In this loss of Self you would ask "Who am I really?' and begin to search for a way to become more conscious of who you are, what life is and what others actually are, to find an understandable context for all the pain so that you could lessen it and maximize the sharing of love.

I could go on with this exercise but it illustrates the huge difference between existing in a world alone versus a world full of relating to others. The difference is the amount of self-knowledge and awareness that is developing. It's important to note that this self-knowledge is not growing just in you and no one else . . . it is growing collectively. As we interact with others we cause them to grow in awareness just as they cause us to grow. We evolve together. It's a co-evolutionary process! We do it by ourselves but we don't do it alone!

MY PERSONAL AWAKENING TO CO-EVOLUTION

Let me expand on this concept of Co-evolution by sharing a direct experience I was blessed to have many years ago. I was in a meditation session as a student in the Rosicrucian Order that was deepened years later at a retreat called the Enlightenment Intensive. These experiences are not unique. They can be found scattered throughout spiritual literature, as I will illustrate below.

I was, on both occasions, intensely contemplating the question "What is life?' trying to directly perceive its essential nature, when all of a sudden I lost the sense of myself as an independent self. I became conscious of myself as the Being of all Beings . . . the Universal Being behind all of existence, everywhere, in all things physical, non-physical, and in everything manifested even in that which dwelt in pure potential. It was expansive, exhilarating and I felt as if the purest light was pouring through me and radiating out of my body. I was paradoxically god and me at the same moment. I was that universal essence but at the same time I was my individual self. I was non-dual but at the same time singular. There was no one else in the universe but me. I was it. I was god and god was me.

I was there just before creation. I was alone wondering if there was anyone else out in the universe. I was aware of a fundamental capability of my true nature . . . I had free choice. In fact I was choice itself. In that state of aloneness I noticed that I had the ability to know everything but in fact knew nothing about myself even though the capacity of infinite self-knowledge was there. I was innocently un-self-aware but the very first instance of self-awareness was: I became aware that I was not self-aware.

Out of my free choice, I chose to ask the question "Who am I?" and I realized that to answer that question, I needed something outside of myself to see myself as a mirror. At that instant I split myself into an infinite number of other individuals with each individual being the same god that I was. They were the same universal god as me with the same infinite potential but each one had an individual point of view. They were like me in that each one of them was me, yet didn't have the same awareness of their individual selves and each other. We were fully conscious but had no knowledge of ourselves, just like how a new born baby is fully conscious but has no experiential knowledge of its new world. We had the capacity to view and reflect back to one another our differentiated perspective but the singularity of each of us as individuals was vitally important. We needed to be slightly different from one another, to accentuate and reflect back to one another each unique aspect of our god self. If we were all the same, we could not notice all these aspects and become more conscious.

In this differentiated state, we could see one another in ways we could not see ourselves. In our difference we could, over eons of time, come to know the totality of our universality. And in order to evolve the knowledge of our god nature we needed one important dynamic: to interact in such a way that we could bring each other to greater consciousness. So we began to relate to one another. It took eons but over time through experimentation we developed a method of doing this: something called communication.

We were one being divided into many unique individuals, relating to one another and creating as many ways as possible to communicate to one another for the sole (soul) purpose of becoming conscious of our true nature. We were doing this all together: co-evolving.

This Enlightenment experience was not unique to me. It is echoed throughout much of ancient and modern spiritual literature. Here are some writings on this subject.

> *"The Sufis often quote the hadith, or extra-Qur'anic revelation, in which God says, 'I was a hidden treasure; I loved to be known, so I created all.' God wants to know (His) nature, (His) possibilities, (His) manifestations. This love to know (Him)self, the desire to know (Him)self, appears in us as the love to inquire . . . One way of understanding*

the situation is that God's love of revealing the divine manifestation appears in us as love for the Truth. These two loves are the same thing; for ultimately there is only one, undivided reality . . . This clarifies what the ultimate service is. You do not work on yourself to become Enlightened; you work on yourself so that God can do what God wants to do, which is to reveal (Him)self. So our delight in investigating reality is an adventure of consciousness, which is the human participation in God's enjoyment of self-revelation."

—Almaas

"We are the means by which the universe is getting to know itself."

—Thomas Berry

"Far away in the heavenly abode of the great god Indra, there is a wonderful net which has been hung by some cunning artificer in such a manner that it stretches out infinitely in all directions. In accordance with the extravagant tastes of deities, the artificer has hung a single glittering jewel in each "eye" of the net, and since the net itself is infinite in dimension, the jewels are infinite in number. There hang the jewels, glittering like stars in the first magnitude, a wonderful sight to behold. If we now arbitrarily select one of these jewels for inspection and look closely at it, we will discover that in its polished surface there are reflected all the other jewels in the net, infinite in number. Not only that, but each of the jewels reflected in this one jewel is also reflecting all the other jewels, so that there is an infinite reflecting process occurring."

—Francis Harold Cook, Hua-Yen Buddhism: *The Jewel Net of Indra*

"In the beginning, that which Is, is all there was and there was nothing else. Yet All That Is could not know itself— because All That Is is all there was, and there was nothing else. . . . Yet the experience of itself is that for which it *longed . . . so All that is divided itself—becoming in one glorious moment, that which is 'this' and that which is 'that' . . . Now in creating that which is 'here' and that which is 'there', God made it possible for God to know Itself. In the moment of this great explosion from within, God created relativity—the greatest gift God ever gave to Itself. Thus, relationship is the greatest gift God ever gave to you."*

—Neal Donald Walsh—*Conversations with God*

"All forms of life and being are simply variations on a single theme: we are all in fact one being doing the same thing in as many different ways as possible."

—Alan Watts, *Does it Matter?*

AWAKENING WITHIN SUFFERING

For months after this initial awakening I had additional insights into our Co-evolutionary universe (these corollary epiphanies often accompany an Enlightenment experience). I became aware that if we were all individual gods each expressing the infinite potentialities of the Universal God, obviously we had the potential for infinite power. I questioned what would happen if these divine individuals began relating to one another without the awareness that they had such power. I looked to the planet for an example.

It was clear what would happen, because it was already happening. There were all manners of relating: from despicable and evil depravity to beautiful and elevated sacredness. There were all manner of personalities from Hitlers, Ida Amins, Stalins to Gandhis, Martin Luther Kings and Mother Teresas. There was extreme victimization of the poor, raping of the environment and slaughter of the helpless. Yet there was great philanthropy, sacred arts and music to uplifting spiritual practices. It became clear that in our unawareness of each other as divine beings with infinite power, we manipulated and overpowered one another. We did not fully know what we were doing and how we affected each other. In our innocence we inflicted terrible suffering and trauma. We experienced the mosh-pit of bashing into one another in the victim/perpetrator game, trapped in the terrible confusion of it all.

But at some point we began to wake up. Down through the ages, in our countless interactions, we communicated the effects of our manipulation and injury to each other. As our communications were completed, we learned to understand. We emerged from our trauma and healing began. We stared across in horror at the person we just shot in war. And maybe we returned back in another life and they shot us. We learned that others are not just objects; they are just as real inside as we are to ourselves. We took the risk to really make contact with one another on a deeper level and discover the divine love that we all intensely feel for each other.

Incrementally, we will learn that we are all interconnected and entwined in this inevitable relationship called Life where the only activity that matters in matter is the communication of ourselves . . . and with every action of relating the most amazing thing is happening . . . we are evolving in self-awareness, love and ability. At some point we will get that it's all sacred, emerging from the mosh-pit of life and moving into a divine square dance finally realizing that we are all gods playing a hide-and-seek game, with you hiding in me and me hiding in you.

> *"Forgive them for they know not what they do"*
> —Jesus Christ

So Co-evolution is a condition of life. It is part of the nature of existence whether we know it or not. It does not depend on us knowing it is happening for it to happen. Co-evolution is occurring if we have a guru or don't have a guru. It's happening if we are on a spiritual path or not. It's happening even if we try to avoid life by running away and living in the woods. We will still be in relationship, even if it's an avoidance relationship. We are all evolving together with the rest of everything else evolving in the universe in an interconnected web.

Once we view life through this lens of Co-evolution, it becomes clear. Does not our greatest personal growth occur in close relationships? Of course! It is why we are drawn to be in groups, friendships and intimate relationships because it's in the relating in these collectives and pairings that the inherent purpose of life, which is to expand our consciousness, is fulfilled. That's where it expands the most. Just like all streams naturally flow together into rivers, and rivers naturally flow together into lakes and oceans, so do we naturally want to converge and communicate ourselves in relationships. So, too, in our true nature, our natural flow is to become more conscious of others and ourselves. This is not a passive activity. It is an active process. We are doing it full-on whether we are aware of co-evolving or not. We cannot escape it. Just as a fish cannot live out of water, we can not exist without others.

When we let the *ah-ha* of this insight settle in, it will radically change our lives. How? Not by altering it or changing it but by all of us accepting the way it actually is. This acceptance transforms our life by bringing us into harmony with the nature of life. Every bit of life is spiritual unfoldment. There is no difference between ordinary life and the spiritual path. This difference is just a mental construct. Every time we complete a communication to another and receive someone else's communication we are not only singularly contributing to the uplifting of ourselves and that other, but we are incrementally contributing to the Co-evolution of the vast web of creation. To see this is to realize the vast importance of each one of us in the U-N-I-verse and our contribution to the massive unfoldment on the planet. Life is where it is all happening. This is IT. It's all sacred . . . the whole shebang, you, me, them, and everything. We are the saviours to each other! We are our own gurus!

So if Co-evolution is what is going on in life then is there a way of enhancing this process so that we evolve and reach Enlightenment much faster? Is there a way that we can heal the suffering that our lack of awareness of each other has caused? The answer to both is yes. To fully answer this we will have to understand more specifically how Co-evolution operates and then we can apply this knowledge to accelerating the process.

> *"Mother I have sought truth and I have learned that all living things create new traditions when they honour the sacredness found in the individual as well as in the whole of creation. I have experienced the clarity of their knowing when they desire understanding as much as they desire the breath of life"*
> —Jamie Sams—*Thirteen Original Clan Mother*

CHAPTER_11

COMMUNICATION AND CO-EVOLUTION

Let us first explore how self-knowledge and understanding develops within the Co-Evolutionary universe so that we can look at how this natural process can be enhanced. Without going too deeply into the philosophy of cognition or how we come to know anything, I am going to suggest some ideas (at the risk of presenting more dogma). Once again these ideas are subject to your own investigation. (I advise you at some point to do the Thought Clearing exercise on "Knowledge" in the back section to come up with your own ideas.)

From my observation of life, I have seen that Co-evolution occurs in a cycle that starts with a conscious decision to relate and moves through contact, speaking, listening and then mutual understanding. After the cycle is complete, it ends or begins again. Let's investigate this cycle together.

THE DECISION TO RELATE

There are many individuals in life. There are billions of them. We pass by many of them on the streets, at work, in restaurants, in parks, etc. They are everywhere but we do not relate to them all. The majority of people in life we overlook. Within the context of Co-evolution however, we are all here for one reason: we want to relate to others in order to become more conscious. This is a given. It is the nature of life. It's the way it is. If someone is in life, they inherently want to relate to others even though they may be unconscious of this fact. We are lucky because there are so many but it is hard to engage with all of them.

So we start off with a thought in the mind that we'd like to get across to another person. There is something about us that we would like another to become conscious of. Because that thought has not been delivered to another person, it is suspended in our mind. We all have had this experience of something we really wanted to say to another person and because it has not been said it keeps circulating around and around in our mind. We start off by choosing someone (or a group of others) to relate to. Even though we are not conscious of the purpose of being in life with all others, we consciously choose a particular someone with which to engage. I look over at Betty and think, "I am going to talk to her now". Now Betty can choose to relate to me or not. She has a choice, too. If she doesn't want to relate with me, then communication cannot occur. Some people actually miss this fact. Sometimes they force or manipulate others to relate to them when the other really doesn't want to.

Fred wants to be by himself to figure out what's going on inside and Jenny keeps telling him what she thinks is going on. He doesn't want to talk. But she keeps trying to get him to talk. Eventually he gets so angry, he tells her off and walks out. This can cause a lot of problems when this happens: abuse, resentment, acting out, anger, sadness, etc. So it's important to understand that people mutually choose to relate to each other. This is where Co-evolution all starts.

CONTACT

The next thing that happens is we decide to connect with the person. We contact them. I go over to Betty in the office; I put my attention on her and try to get her attention: "Hello there". If she in turn chooses to interact with me then she puts her attention on me. We put our attention on one another relative to our current awareness of each other. If I think that Betty is just a body, I put my attention on her as a body. If I think that Betty is more than just a body, that she is a real conscious individual, I put my attention on her as this. If I think that she is divine in nature, then I put my attention on her as that. Anyone who has interacted with a very holy person can sense the qualitative difference between someone seeing you as just a body and someone seeing you as divine. So we establish some level of rapport with them based on our present awareness of what others are.

Within this contact there are 2 choices: the choice to trust and to be open. The trust is two-fold: trust of others and trust of oneself. Betty may have had some interactions with men that were not so good so she may be suspicious of me, being a man, and not trust me completely. Then again, there may be something in my authenticity that she feels safe with and as a result chooses to take the risk to trust a bit more than she normally does. But she may also have a high level of ability to communicate to men and therefore trust that if the communication gets weird she can manage to extract herself from it. So she may not trust me but she is confident of her ability to make the interaction safe for herself. Her trust is higher than one who has a lower level of ability to interact with men.

According to the degree that we feel safe with others and our own ability to create safety, we then choose to be fully open, less open or closed to others. I may decide to be fully open to Betty but she may be suspicious of me if I am a stranger and decide to be less open than me. Depending on our openness with one another, we decide how much of ourselves we want to share or how authentic and real we want to be. The reality of ourselves is often the most delicate, tenuous and sensitive parts of our being. Once again, this is all dependent on choice. Each one of us decides to connect with others to the degree that we choose to trust and be open to one another. The choice to contact another to be open and trust cannot be forced upon us by others. When we honour another's choice to relate to us or not and they recognize this, we automatically start off with more openness and trust.

It is important to note that there is a field of two opposites in which we choose. Will we be rejected or will we be overwhelmed by others? These are the two fundamental fears of life. If we are not accepted by others, we will end up being alone. On the other hand, if others overpower us too much, we will close down and contract within ourselves. We will withdraw from others and also end up being alone. (This is the trauma experience that we explored in the chapter on Barriers to Awakening.) In both cases, we end up back in the original state of being in "solitary confinement" in the universe unable to become conscious. We do not want to be solitary in the universe because we need others in our long journey of awakening to become conscious. Being alone is contrary to this purpose. This is where the whole big-bang started in the first place and we don't want to go back to square one.

SPEAKING

Once contact with another is established, we translate our internal experience into words and get them across to others. Let's say I have had an experience of being outside in the cold when it has been hailing out. In order to successfully communicate, I first go through a process of constructing my message. I start by placing my attention on the full experience, noting all of its components. I make distinctions between all the elements. There is being outside, being hit by hail, wind, wetness, body sensations of coldness, shivering, the colour and size of the hail, etc. I go through a process of associating all of these with prior experiences in my memory, searching for individual words and concepts connected to these and then compose my message. This inner contemplation may take only a second or take a longer period of silence. Once it is done, I communicate in words using the appropriate body language and vocal inflections to get across my experience to Betty: "It's god-awful cold out there. The wind is blowing around hailstones the size of baseballs. I'm wet and shivering!" Even though words are merely a representation of my experience, I try to get across my experience with words.

LISTENING

The listener, being open, then receives the thoughts that were communicated. This involves an inner process, as well, of sorting and constructing. Betty hears my message and distinguishes all the separate names and concepts in my communication. There is a sorting process of drawing up from memory her experiences of coldness, wind, shivering, wetness, etc and then she puts these all back together into a composite image that matches what I communicated. When she does this, she may actually have a similar experience to me. When there is a match between my representation and Betty's, we can say that mutual understanding or consciousness has occurred. What I communicated and what she received are the same.

ACKNOWLEDGEMENT

The communication cycle however does not end here. There needs to be recognition on the speaker's part that the listener understood the communication. In some way, the receiver needs to indicate to the speaker that they understood what was communicated. We may indicate this with a nod, a smile, saying "I got it" or "I understand" or by repeating back what was said or a number of other ways. Betty may say: "Wow, you really got hit by bad weather; let me get you a blanket to get warm". So when I see that Betty received exactly what I communicated about myself, then there is mutual understanding. She received exactly the thoughts that I sent and I recognize that she received them.

When mutual understanding occurs, a magical thing happens. The thought that I started off with that was hanging in my mind disappears. It is no longer occupying my attention. It is gone and there is now more space in my consciousness. The minor tension behind the desire to be understood by another has been relieved. I may feel closer to Betty and perhaps some deeper communication can happen as a result. We have recognized a new experience, made new connections in the mind and expanded our awareness of one another incrementally. There is a sense of fulfillment in this basic act of becoming a little bit more conscious of one another because that is what life is about. We feel an inherent sense of satisfaction when we learn anything new or acquire a new skill. In a similar way, when we understand another person, there is that same feeling that we are fulfilling the purpose of life in our interaction.

Now what would have happened if I did not get my communication across to Betty? What if Betty just ignored me? My thoughts would have stayed suspended in my mind and because it is our natural tendency to want to relate to others, I would have to use some of my internal energy to hold that communication back. My thoughts would be pushed into the area of my mind where all the other uncommunicated thoughts are crowded and, like a computer that slows down when thousands of e-mails are stored in the outbox, my effectiveness as a person would be compromised.

This is the fundamental reason why we suffer in life. To one degree or another we have been traumatized, criticized, ignored, forced, or hurt by others who are not fully conscious of who we really are, because they are not fully conscious of who they really are. We have not been given the safety and opportunity to have another person understand our experience of these overwhelming events and the only thing we can do is hold back our thoughts and emotions with any number of coping mechanisms: denial, suppression, fogging, minimalization, shame, etc. We have to do something to hold these communications back: take on a 'nice' personality and be the way mother wants us to be, make up a fictional explanation of 'I'm unlovable' to explain father's harsh criticalness or create a false solution of being sad like grandma hoping it will take her depression away. It takes a lot of energy to bury these communications. But they do not die. They get buried and stay alive. There is a reactive charge to them and when we meet people and experiences similar to those from the past, this charge gets released and it creates further havoc in our relationships.

Yet the potential to complete our communications is eternally there because, as we explored, if anyone is in life then they are here to relate and evolve in relationships. We are compelled, unavoidably, from the very essence of our divine nature, to get closer to one another.

Deep down inside we are yearning to heal our past and be understood and to find people and circumstances where we can do this. When we find these special people, we can choose to risk again, be open, get our withheld communications across, be received and achieve mutual understanding.

If enough mutual understanding occurs with a few people, affinity and love develops. We can start to feel safe to share the more vulnerable aspects of ourselves. More satisfying engagement happens, allowing us to not only process and let go of our withheld pain but take the risk to investigate and communicate to each other the profound mystery of our true nature.

Under special circumstances such as an extended retreat where communication between individuals is structured so that people are being understood and consistently completing deeper levels of authentic relating, we can extricate ourselves from our socialized personality and heal our deepest traumas. As the ego masks then fall away and we are being seen as we really are, then the real possibility of recognizing our true nature is available. Direct experience can occur and when it does, the mind is massively transformed. The fiction from which we have been living is annihilated. Truth is realized and becomes the basis upon which we can start living a new life.

THE COMMUNICATION CYCLE

In conclusion, it appears that Co-evolution moves through a fundamental process that starts with a decision to relate and contact then progresses through a cycle of:

1. Sending thoughts or communicating after a brief period of contemplation
2. Receiving thoughts or listening
3. Acknowledgement or mutual understanding.

> *"Knowing together produces a new level of surprise . . . a brand new Awareness."*
> —Richard Chester, PhD

What this means is that every individual act of being understood or understanding others is a spiritual act. Receiving and giving the authentic message of ourselves to one another is a small sacrament in the service of our own evolution . . . an act that we overlook, in our deep desire, to live an exalted spiritual existence. This ordinary act of everyday life could be evolving us far more than the solitary spiritual practices that we've assumed are the only way to awakening.

So if relating to one another is fundamental to the development of consciousness, the next question is this: is it possible to speed-up this process of co-evolution so that we can evolve in self-awareness more rapidly than in normal life. Is it possible to use this process so that we can come to our own insights and awakening without the influence of a dogmatic guru? The exciting answer is "Yes" and that is the subject for the next chapter.

CHAPTER 12

CO-EVOLUTION AND
THE DYAD TECHNIQUE

We ended the last chapter with a question of whether or not we can speed up the process of Co-evolution so that we can grow in self-consciousness much faster than in life. Can we take this natural dynamic and duplicate or arrange it in some way that it is still doing its thing of evolution but more rapidly? Yes we can and to do this we have to improve two aspects: the quantity and quality of relating. We need to do this by enhancing the way that co-evolution occurs (as discussed in the last chapter): through a communication cycle.

QUANTITY AND QUALITY OF RELATING

It goes without saying that the more communications that are completed between individuals, the greater the mutual understanding and therefore the greater the self-awareness. This is fairly obvious: more completed relating equals more personal insight.

The second aspect, quality of relating, is not so obvious, but it has to do with the authenticity of the communication.

There are two ways in which we communicate our experience. The first is presentational, which is poetical and non-explanatory. It might be in words, but it might also be a laugh, a cry, a furrowed brow, or even a momentary diversion of the eyes. We are acutely sensitive to non-verbal messages from others and tend to react to these in a gut-level manner that is largely unconscious and emotional. The second mode is discursive, which is, by contrast, prosaic and explanatory and it necessarily engages our logical and discursive minds. Discursive communication is the story or explanation, of what we think and how we feel. It is the picture painted in words.

Good actors know how to present themselves in a convincing manner, so that their presentational and discursive communications are in synch. The result is very satisfying for an audience. We enjoy watching them and we are taken up in the story.

When these two modes of communication are at odds with each other, however, we experience the communication of the other as *non-authentic* and this experience is distinctly unsettling. Suppose we are listening to someone whose brow is furrowed tightly, who is periodically clenching their teeth and whose whole manner appears to be tense and angry. If what they say is: "My mother is a wonderful person," we experience a certain degree of frustration because we have not received an authentic or complete communication and we are not convinced.

Authenticity is also the condition where the outer presentation of a person to another corresponds to their inner experience. In other words we can say they are being "real". They are honestly presenting externally what it is that they are thinking, feeling and sensing inside. They are being genuine. When they say they are sad they are actually feeling sad and not only that but presenting being in sadness. When they say they are excited they don't just say the words "I'm excited" descriptively, but they act excited.

The authenticity factor is extremely important in the co-evolution process. In order for us to come to a true realization about ourselves, we need to be in touch with the truth of ourselves and tell the truth.

To hide, avoid, cover up or tell a lie only reinforces the illusion we are trapped in. Phony relating does not produce real insights. To know the truth, we need to tell the truth. It's the deal that reality has made with us though unfortunately many of us miss it and it is one of central challenges that we all face in life: being true to ourselves, being ourselves around others and feeling okay about being real. So the enhancement of authenticity is an important factor.

So how do we improve the quantity and quality of relating?

Here's what we do. We create the co-evolutionary universe in microcosmic form, structure the relating and add in agreements that facilitate the quantity and quality of relating with an understanding of what hinders and enhances the process. That's a mouthful so let's go into the method. This method is called the dyad and it's a method I have been using in my work for over 30 years.

THE DYAD STRUCTURE
The Universe in Microcosm

Because we know that co-evolution occurs when one person communicates to another in a cycle of communication (sending, receiving and acknowledgement), we can create a structure that allows for this process to unfold. This basic unit is simple: a listener and a speaker without obtuse esotericism, sacred geometry or gurus, just a couple of human beings. This is a called a "dyad" meaning two, and in this case, two people. First, we set this up physically, with two individuals sitting directly across from one another, a comfortable distance apart, facing and looking at each other. Second, we get the two individuals to agree to certain behavioural procedures and agreements that ensure the completion of the communication cycle.

As we explored in the last chapter under the section on contact, we need to trust others and ourselves in order to open up to and deepen our contact with others. We need to be assured it will be safe to be who we really are. It is very difficult to open up to one another in a chaotic universe if we cannot predict how others will treat us if we do. Therefore, we need to establish ahead of time our rules of engagement so that we know what to expect when we take the risk to express the reality of our experience to others.

These agreements and procedures give each person a gradually deepening sense of security and emotional safety so that they can go more deeply into their experience and reveal this reality to each other.

NON-INTERRUPTION

The first essential agreement is non-interruption. If communication is to be completed, then one person has to listen and one person has to speak. The two people cannot be speaking at the same time. Interruption is the constant bane that breaks down everyday conversation. Sometimes we don't even listen to people; we are just listening for a pause in the other person's sentence so that we can get in our two cents' worth. Interruption often aggravates a heated discussion into a fiery argument when people get frustrated that they cannot get their point across. If we observed how much interruption occurs, we would find it amazing that any conversations ever got completed.

So we need to set up the structure so one person agrees to listen and the other person agrees to speak without interruption. We can do this by giving the speaker a limited period of time to speak and then after this time have the roles change over and let the listener become the speaker and communicate for the same length of time. An optimal period of time is roughly 5 minutes. This can be done with a stopwatch or a timer that beeps at the end of each interval to indicate the changeover. These alternating 5-minute changeovers can be for 40 minutes, back and forth.

CONFIDENTIALITY

The next agreement is common in most self-help groups: confidentiality. We need to concur that whatever is said in the dyad between the two people is not shared anywhere else, outside the dyad . . . not to anyone else, in any other space, under any circumstance . . . ever. Even the names of the people we shared with should not be mentioned to anyone else outside the dyad or outside the group doing dyads.

NON-EVALUATION

Thirdly, we need to agree that we will refrain from expressing criticism, either positive or negative, either verbally or non-verbally of what another is presenting or describing. Non-evaluative listening is not the same as empathic listening or mirroring, where the listener attempts to ally themselves with the speaker by responding empathically to their communication. The dyad is not therapy or peer counseling. It is more like an experimental laboratory where we are creating the best conditions for the emergence of self-insight.

The non-evaluation agreement is not easy to keep since it is almost entirely foreign to our everyday experience. We may find it extremely difficult, when listening to another, to refrain from making our private judgments. Does what they are saying make sense or not? Do we feel the same way as they do or not? Do we find it interesting or boring? Even when we are listening intently to another, our minds are working overtime.

But it is very important that we try, to the very best of our ability, to suspend judgments of another. If that is impossible, then we must try our best to avoid communicating our judgments, either verbally or non-verbally. A furrowed brow, a downward tilt of the chin or a grim set of the mouth may communicate to others that what they are saying is not acceptable. Their response may be to shut down or to cut short their communication. If unconscious behavioural patterns have been triggered, they may do the opposite—communicate reactively to us as the listener. Either way, our perceived negative evaluation of them will create a reaction and distract them from open contemplation.

Even when we agree with what they are saying, it is important to remain neutral. A positive evaluation can subtly reinforce the speaker's false personality instead of opening the space for them to present how they really are and, for example, the speaker may think: "they have complimented me on being funny and I guess they like that so I won't really tell them I am having a rough time."

Eliminating judgment creates an environment where the quality of relating, or authenticity, can be cultivated. Individuals will feel safe to look inside and openly express the truth of themselves freely and honestly.

NON-INFLUENCE

This agreement is related to the non-evaluation agreement. As listeners, we should avoid trying to help the person find the right words or do anything that assists the person to communicate to us. We should just listen and not speak. It is tempting to help a person when they are struggling to find the right words but this struggle is actually helping them develop their ability to make the associations of inner experience to language so they can improve their ability to communicate in life to others. If we help them, they are denied the valuable opportunity to evolve this capacity. As listeners, we should also avoid nodding or smiling or laughing. This eliminates the often-subtle cues that socialize us to be a certain way. By nodding or smiling we are often non-verbally saying to the speaker: "I like what you are saying . . . say more" or "be the way I'm liking you to be right now" and this prevents the person from looking inside to find their own personal truth rather than conform to what the listener likes. Some people will find the avoidance of nodding or smiling difficult, even thinking it is impolite, but when we understand how we unconsciously manipulate each other to be nice or sociable through these habitual subtle cues, we can offer this gift of non-influence to others. When we are on the receiving end of someone just listening, without responding, we will experience the wonderful gift of time, within the presence of another, to look inside and find out what is true for us rather than what is true for others. For some people this is a revolution in their life: to be allowed for the first time to go into the inner sanctum of themselves and have a glimpse of their real essence.

FULL ATTENTION

Because the way that the evolution of self-awareness evolves is through mutual understanding, it is crucially important that we, as the listener, try to fully understand what the person is saying. We should be in a space of non-judgmental openness to what the speaker is presenting. Our main intention is to fully understand what the speaker is communicating.

We should put our full attention on the speaking partner even if the speaking person closes their eyes to silently contemplate for a while. We should maintain eye contact with the person at all times whether the person is talking or silent. We should try to avoid being distracted by our own thoughts while we are listening so we can be fully present for our partner. This is very difficult, since people commonly think about other things when other people are talking, so we need not be discouraged when we space out or lose concentration. If this happens, we can simply say: "Say that again" or "Say that again louder" if we missed a phrase or two, or "Summarize that" if the person has said a lot and we weren't sure what the essence was of what the person was trying to say. We, as the listener, could also say, "Clarify _____" adding in the sentence or terminology that we didn't understand. These simple instructions can vastly improve the chances of communication getting completed.

At the end of the timed period of 5 minutes, when the beeper or bell from the timer goes off, as a listener we just say a simple "Thank you" to indicate that we have understood.

This form of full listening has a powerful effect on the speaker. When we listen in this manner, we are adding our attention energy to the speaker's attention energy, so they actually have more energy to go within and contemplate their inner dimension. They will be able to touch into their subtler inner realm more clearly with that extra energy. Our attention, in addition, helps keep them on track with their own inquiry because the speaker knows that we are there waiting for a communication from them, unlike in solitary meditation where beginning meditators can spend 70-80% of their time spacing out and losing track of their object of concentration.

Full attention is also powerful in the sense that it non-verbally communicates to the speaker "I care", "I have a regard for you", and "I have compassion for you". Within the warmth of that open space of non-judgment, non-interference, non-interruption and confidentiality, we can allow ourselves and others to gradually let down defensives, to be more authentic and real and to say what has been true for many years and has never been said or received by another. There is great potential to let go of the suspended communications and the frozen suffering that has held us back in life, allowing profound healing and insights to occur.

This caring contact is similar in quality to the same contact that we may experience or search for in a guru. As we do more and more dyads with the same person or different people, we will experience the same divine rapport and connection that we look for in the spiritual teacher. And if we think about this, why shouldn't we? Do we all not arise from the same divine source as a realized teacher? Only in this situation we are allowing ourselves to be each other's guru. As I said earlier, the saviour is us.

SELF-REFERENCING

There are also important agreements we need to follow when it is our turn to speak. To make communication more genuine and authentic, we need to confine it to the reality of our personal experience, for that is the only experience about which we can claim any direct knowledge. Sometimes in a conversation, we use the generic form of "you". For example, one might say, "you know when you go to the store and you have to choose between two types of lettuce and you can't decide and you just feel so stupid?" This is a way of speaking about us, or people in general, in a theoretical way. When we speak in this general way we can run the risk of our partner sitting across from us, thinking we are talking about them and feeling evaluated. There can be some confusion in the listener's mind about whether or not we are referring to them or not. "Is he/she thinking I'm stupid"? This confusion can remain suspended in the mind and can be a source of upset if the listener takes it personally. It is much better for us as the speaker to own what we are saying and refer to ourselves using "I" statements. "When I go to the store, I have a hard time making a choice between 2 types of lettuce and I feel stupid". This is very clear with no possible reference to the partner. Use of the universal "we" is okay, e.g. "We all want love", but a person should distinguish if the reference is really about them, e.g. "I want love" and own that. Self-referencing creates an environment of greater authenticity and truthfulness where people are speaking more from their real self. When this quality of relating or authenticity is enhanced, co-evolution is enhanced as well.

Another aspect of self-referencing is to avoid referring to what your partner said when it's their turn to speak. There is an element of resonance that occurs as people share more intimately their inner landscape with one another. We may see a likeness of another to ourselves as they speak about a life experience. We may have an *aha* moment as they talk about themselves and then all of a sudden we have an important insight about our case in life. The temptation is to say something like, "Wow, I totally relate to what you said. God I have such a hard time choosing what lettuce to buy and, like you, I feel stupid". We should avoid referring to our partner especially in the way of making comparisons or offering similarities or differences. To do this runs the risk, once again, of offering an unintended evaluation that could be upsetting or even devastating to our partner. It is much better to let go of what the partner just said in their turn and go into silence and contemplate our subject of interest and come up with something about ourselves. If what does surface is related to what our partner said, we should phrase it as originating in ourselves, in our own words, in the way that it is uniquely our experience. "You know there are times when I go to the Farmers' Market and I just get overwhelmed with all the choices and it just reminds me of how overwhelmed I am in my life. There are just too many decisions. I wish the world would stop".

As we engage in the dyad with these agreements, there will be a short adjustment period because the format is different from usual relating. We should realize that we have a different purpose than social conversation, peer support or counseling. Our goal is not to get along, have fun, entertain, convince or help one another, although these are all worthy endeavours. The goal of the dyad exercise is to enhance communication so we can help each other to evolve. Once we experience the power of this profound process, we will experience the deep fulfillment of mutual understanding and self-awareness.

> "A mind that conforms to any pattern of authority, inward or outward, cannot be sensitive. It is only when a mind is really sensitive, alert, aware of all its own happenings, responses, thoughts, when it is no longer becoming, no longer shaping itself to be something, only then is it capable of receiving truth. It is only then there can be happiness, for happiness is not an end—it is the result of reality."
> —J Krishnamurti

PREPARATION BEFORE THE DYAD BEGINS

Now that the physical and non-physical structure is set-up, the communication process can proceed. It is best to begin with a topic or focus that we can inquire into.

Before the communication starts, we should choose something that we want to investigate rather than just communicating random thoughts on any subject. We do not all have to choose the same subject. These subjects could be about gaining personal insights, e.g. how we want to be loved, problem resolution, clarifying concepts (what is a guru?) or working towards awakening, e.g. "Who am I?" or "What is life?" A list of the subjects of inquiry is provided at the end of this book. It is best that we choose a subject that is of interest since that sense of interest will empower your inquiry. So you are to choose an area related to Self, life or another and then tell the other what that topic is. (Sometimes there could be 2 or 3 subjects of the inquiry, as indicated in the exercise portion of the book)

The questions are phrased in terms of an instruction such as: "Tell me who you are" or "Tell me some concerns you have about being yourself around others". An instruction is much better than a question such as "Who are you?" It gives a directive to the mind and indicates what we should do. "Who are you" does not elicit such a response. An instruction does. There is a qualitative difference between a question and an instruction. If the inquiry is put into question form—e.g. "Who are you?"—there is no directive and, in some instances, the question can feel mildly intrusive or confrontational. An instruction is more neutral. The question should be put into an instructional form and then given to the partner.

Once we understand what our respective instructions are, we let our partners know our instruction(s) and decide who is to receive the questions first. We are now ready to start the dyad.

THE DYAD PROCESS IN OPERATION
The Communication Cycle

People who are doing a 40-minute dyad with each other should first of all have in place a means of marking off successive 5-minute periods, either through the use of a timer or the use of a CD that marks off the eight 5-minute periods with a gong or other sound.

STEP ONE: GIVING AND RECEIVING AN INSTRUCTION

The speaker gives the listener their instruction in the "Tell me . . ." format. The wording of the instruction should stay the same as it is repeated and there are no insertions or additions. Speakers should not say "So, um, tell me who you are" and they should not say, "Charles, tell me who you are". They should simply say: "Tell me who you are" directly, as one uninterrupted thought.

The speaker should receive the question as fully as possible, allowing the question to settle into themselves, into their body, in such a way that it can start to direct their contemplation

STEP TWO: CONTEMPLATION

Once the person in the role of the speaker receives the question, they should go into silence. They should start their silence with a simple intention to experience the truth of what they are investigating, recognizing their goal, which is to know the essence of what they are inquiring into. They should set out to achieve a deep "knowingness" of what it is they are investigating. If it is a subject of a new understanding, they want to have deep insight into it. If they want to awaken to their true nature, they set out to have a direct experience of their true nature (see the section on Insight and Enlightenment subjects and review the difference between the two states). The intention is to simply establish your goal in place. There is no effort other than a mental decision with the idea that insight or awakening will happen even though you don't know how or when it will occur.

If the person is working on an Enlightenment question, such as "Who am I?", "What is life?" or "What is another?" the person should start the inquiry by placing their attention on the most real "felt sense" of that subject in the moment with the objective of "directly experiencing" who or what that actually is.

For example, if the instruction is: "Tell me who you are", what is most real about the Self at that moment might be an ache in the lower back. It might be a memory of a time with grandpa at the beach. It might be a feeling of tiredness or boredom. It might be a thought, such as "I wonder what's for lunch." Whatever is most real, most present, in relation to the instruction received, this is what is taken as the object of inquiry.

If the instruction is: "Tell me what life is", then the person is to direct their attention to their most real experience of life at that moment. It might be the hearing of a birdcall. It might be their awareness of someone in the room crying. It might be a memory of seeing Uncle Rocky in his coffin. Whatever is most real, most present, in relation to the instruction received, this is what is taken as the object of inquiry.

Similarly, if the question is: "Tell me what another is", the person directs their attention to another person or sentient being. It might be the person sitting next to them. It might be their spouse at home. It might be Jesus Christ. It might be their dog, Buster. Again, whatever is most real, most present, in relation to the instruction received, this is what is taken as the object of inquiry.

The speaker then allows him/herself to just be open to whatever enters consciousness that is the result of the intention. "Openness" is a very broad term, which often is defined in terms of what it is not. It is a space of non-judgment of what enters the mind. One does not try to have anything enter or resist what is coming up in the mind. One does not try to force perceptions, thoughts or feelings to come or manipulate them to leave the mind. It is a space of allowing in a willingness to be surprised by anything that enters into consciousness. What may come up may appear to have nothing to do with the inquiry and this should be accepted. The speaker should just trust that what came up in the contemplation, whether or not it is related to the subject, has some inner rationale for arising. The person should avoid speaking right away when material comes up and instead should sit in silence with it a little while longer as a way of gathering the essence of what it was that occurred.

STEP 3—COMMUNICATION

After the period of contemplation, the speaker is then to locate the words necessary to communicate as accurately as possible what arose in their silent contemplation that was the result of their intention to experience the truth. It might be helpful to think of "presenting" the contents of their experience to the listener, rather than "describing" or "explaining" them. The speaker should use whatever channels of communication they can to get themselves across: words, body language, voice inflection, actions, feelings, etc, so that the listener can fully understand what the speaker experienced. In other words, they should try to be authentic, having the presentation match as closely as possible to what they experienced in the silent contemplation without adding or taking anything away. If there is laughter, sadness, confusion, doubt, dullness, irritation, calmness, excitement, equanimity, etc, the speaker should be in the experience of it and communicate it so that the listening partner can understand it fully. Of course the speaker needs to follow the agreements that we discussed above about non-evaluation and self-referencing.

If at anytime the listener does not understand something that the speaker has said, he/she can use the communication aids described above: "Clarify _____", "Say that again", or "Summarize that". The listener then says "Thank you" and the speaker continues with their contemplation/communication if it is still their turn. If the 5-minute timer has not sounded and the communication is completed, the speaker goes back to Step 2 and contemplates their question again until the 5-minute timer goes off.

STEP 4—ACKNOWLEDGEMENT

When the gong or timer sounds at the end of the five-minute period, the speaker wraps up what they are saying and stops speaking. The listening partner then says "Thank you" as an acknowledgement of understanding all that the speaker has communicated.

If the speaker is working on a subject with two or three instructions, he/she indicates to the listener that he/she is finished working on the instruction and can receive the next instruction. The listener indicates that he/she has understood the speaker by saying "Thank you", then gives the next instruction in the series.

Some instructions have two or three parts, and this type of question presents a different challenge to the speaker. The goal is to cover all two or three parts of the question within the five-minute period, so they will have to time themselves to a certain extent. They will receive the first instruction and then contemplate and communicate their experience as it relates to this part. Their partner will then say "Thank you" and will go to Step One again and give them the next instruction in the series. The speaker will contemplate and communicate their experience as it relates to this part, and so forth. If they have covered all two or three parts of the question and they still have time, then they will go back to receiving the first instruction again in the series and contemplate and communicate anything further that is coming into experience.

STEP 5—ROLE REVERSAL

When the 5-minute timer sounds and the listener has said "Thank you" to the speaker, then the roles reverse and they start again (with the roles reversed) at Step One until the end of the 40-minute period.

SUMMARY

What we have essentially done with this Dyad method is take the natural dynamic of co-evolution already occurring in life and refine it by removing the elements that hinder self-consciousness and enhance the elements that increase it. With the agreements of non-interruption, non-evaluation/confidentiality, self-referencing, non-influence and full attention, we reduce the chances of emotional injury and cultivate an environment where the quality of authenticity or truthfulness of sharing can grow. By structuring the exchange in a "communication cycle" the quantity of relating is increased. People feel safer to share in a deeper, more meaningful way. The open, inviting contact of the listening partner in a unique way reproduces the rapport that we feel with a guru, without having to have a guru. Suspended communications and experiences are completed and profound healing, deep insights and spiritual experiences can occur in a very short period of time for those that practice this technique consistently over a number of days. All of this happens in harmony with the way life actually works. Through this method, the aim of life to evolve in consciousness and ability gets fulfilled in an ongoing way.

Imagine now, the possible outcome of individuals agreeing to do the Co-evolution process in the dyad format over 1-4 days. The growth in Self and life awareness can be quite remarkable and all of this is without the dogmatic influence of the guru. You and I become our own gurus. Here are some reports from some of the participants in Co-evolution retreats I have led:

> *"I discovered a bond linking myself with others, that we are all beings trapped within our minds trying to communicate our fears and need for love. I am becoming more loving, more real, more open, truthful and trustworthy."*
> —Doug Tyler—Real Estate Rep, Toronto, Ontario.

> *"I felt like I accessed the eternal, underlying, universal oneness that we all belong to and create. Half-way through the weekend I found myself sighing a lot. These were not sighs of stress but sighs of bliss. It was my body's way of saying 'yummy, this is sooo delightful, peaceful, and wonderful. The dyad technique is truly the best gift one could give and receive because they're getting themselves. I recommend it to anyone who has a desire to learn more about themselves and life here on earth."*
> —Lise Gillis—Employment Counselor, Kingston, Ontario

> *"I've learned that the greatest gift I can give to others is myself, to give from who I am and not from some false personality or ego"*
> —Steven Kovacs—Lighting sales, Toronto, Ontario

> *"It's like I did 5 years of meditation in one weekend!"*
> —Beth Clark—Yoga and Meditation Teacher, Kingston, Ontario.

One of the most unique applications of the Co-evolution process is a retreat called The Enlightenment Intensive. Relatively unknown in the west (even though it has existed since 1968), it has consistently helped people achieve deep states of awakening in 1 ½ to 4 days. To many, the idea that awakening can occur in this short period may seem unbelievable or even a hoax. For centuries this process has typically taken months or years or even a lifetime in extended periods of solitary meditation. However, if we consider that there has been advancement in so many other areas of life in technology, medicine, astronomy, transportation, etc; can it not be conceivable that improvements can be made to speed up the process of spiritual growth?

Since most individuals in our western, busy lifestyle do not have the time to take weeks or months off to spend in silence, the Co-evolution method and the Enlightenment Intensive makes the prospect of awakening and the benefit of a deeper, more fulfilled life available to a much greater population. Let us explore this method.

CHAPTER 13

THE ENLIGHTENMENT INTENSIVE

Ever since humankind became self-conscious we have sought the answers to explain and understand our existence. Does life have a purpose or is it just a meaningless series of events randomly strung together? Do we as individuals actually exist or are we just part of a dream that someone else is imagining? Do we have a soul or a spirit? Do we exist just for this life or for eternity? Who are we? Is there a real self inside or are we just a personality that is the consequence of all the developmental influences of our upbringing, culture, peer group, etc?

Many religions, superstitions and philosophies have been formed to answer these questions and for most of the world's population, these explanations have been enough and people are satisfied to not dig any deeper. But a growing number of people are beginning to realize that these explanations are only intellectual understandings, they are second hand-beliefs. Many of us long to experience the truth directly for ourselves rather than just be satisfied with someone else's articulation of what Self and life actually is.

Some of us have experienced a degree of suffering in the world or have become disillusioned or disheartened with our existence. As a result we have been motivated to relieve our suffering by seeking to make sense of our lives and understand if there is a deeper experience of Self and a more fulfilled way of living.

Some of us have just moved into a path of yearning for more spiritual experience in our lives as a result of our own natural unfoldment.

And there are some of us who have tried and tried though many methods of awakening and have not fully succeeded. They are ready to give up the search but can't because something deep inside of them keeps tugging at them.

Whatever category we fit into, the Enlightenment Intensive gives us an opportunity to finally become successful in the long search for self-realization without the impediment of a dogma. Through this method, we can truly find the guru within.

WHAT IS AN ENLIGHTENMENT INTENSIVE?

The Enlightenment Intensive is a 4-day retreat that usually begins with supper around 6:30 pm on a Thursday evening and ends after lunch at 2 pm on Monday. On Thursday evening, participants become familiar with each other, the staff, the format, the environment and the technique used on the intensive. Friday, Saturday and Sunday form the main body of the retreat. Monday is an integration period in which participants are guided to bring the benefits of the retreat into their lives. The retreat is typically conducted in a rural, secluded environment. All participants stay and sleep at the facility for the duration of the retreat. Meals are organic (when possible) and vegetarian.

THE PURPOSE

The retreat provides individuals with the optimal opportunity to awaken to the true nature of Self, life and others. In the process, minor or major barriers to one's deeper fulfillment in life can be dissolved so that individuals can engage more fully in all of life's experiences with a deeper connection to themselves and others.

HISTORY

In the 1950's, Charles Berner, an American spiritual teacher (1929-2007) in California, had a powerful awakening experience of the Co-evolutionary principle in life and saw that in our true natures, we are all trying to get closer to one another to fulfill our eternal relationship. He formed the Institute of Ability in California and began researching and developing methods following this principle to help people grow personally.

He set out to improve people's relating ability to improve their lives. When people made agreements of non-interruption, non-evaluation, listener empathy and agreed only to self-reference rather than discuss what other people said, he found that people became more honest, authentic and real. In his initial work, he also noticed that the greatest barrier to personal growth also occurred as the result of incorrect relating. He saw that if the communication between others was injurious, overwhelming, not understood or incomplete, e.g. difficult childhood experiences, then these experiences and the unfulfilled communications were suspended in the mind creating an unconscious reactivity. When people encountered present situations similar to the past, these old experiences were triggered. This reactivity was the primary source of problems in life.

A major part of his work was the development of the dyad technique where partners would take turns as a listener and speaking partner asking each other many different questions and relate within communication guidelines. They were able to complete past unresolved communications and, as a result, they became more problem-free, mentally and emotionally balanced, more alive and engaged, and their life worked better.

THE ADDITION OF INQUIRY

Then in 1968, it occurred to Charles after reading Philip Kapleau's book, "The Three Pillars of Zen," that the dyad format, which had worked so well in other areas of life, might be used to answer life's most important questions.

Charles and his wife Ava gathered their students together and added an inquiry step to the process where the speaking partner would be asked the question, "Who am I?" then go into a meditative silence, put their attention on themselves and intend to directly experience their true nature. They would then communicate what they came up with to the listening partner as they usually did in the former dyad structure.

They were surprised and amazed to find that within a period of just a few days the students were having Enlightenment experiences. They realized soon after that they had taken the best of the Eastern technique of Zen inquiry and added it to the Western technique of relational psychology. A powerful synthesis of the Eastern and Western approaches to personal evolution! They had not only discovered a method to bring people to Enlightenment in a short period of time but a way to help people clear the reactive mind of minor or major barriers in their lives. Charles and Ava further refined the format over about 50 intensives before they felt they had the final form.

The 4-day format was optimal, anything less did not allow enough time for the emptying of the mind and the deepening of awakening through the communication part of the technique. They called the retreat the Enlightenment Intensive.

WHAT IS ENLIGHTENMENT?

Enlightenment has had many names throughout history depending on the tradition: "awakening", "illumination", "transcendence", "self-realization", "kensho" in Zen, "anubhava" in Hinduism" and "unitive consciousness" in modern psychology. Although there may be many opinions of what the phenomena is, this is the understanding of Enlightenment as it occurs on the retreat: **Enlightenment is the direct experience of the true nature of Self, life or others.**

"Direct experience", as we explored earlier, is beyond all the indirect methods we commonly depend on for knowing: sensing, thinking, learning, deciding, reasoning, or feeling. It is beyond intellectual understanding and belief. Direct experience also means to be in union.

For a brief moment in time we are no longer separated from our real essence. We are united. We are one with ourselves. We are "real-I-zed".

"True nature" encompasses the essence of who we are, what life and others are, beyond the mind, emotions and body, the one that we were born as, before all the influences of personal history and before the ego formed due to the socialization of family, friends, school, job, culture and society and the developmental influences of pain, trauma and abuse.

With direct experience, we unite with our true nature in a timeless instant, a spontaneous 'aha' flash that lights up our whole being in such a way that we experience the magnificence of the true self, but also know with absolute certainty, without a doubt, the fact of our true being. The awareness is self-evident and as a result we drop more of the false personality that we have been trapped in and come home to the authentic natural self. We are more able to present ourselves from this state. It is a simple, exhilarating and revitalizing life-altering spiritual experience accompanied by a deep sense of peace, serenity, bliss and inner harmony.

CO-EVOLUTION METHOD IN THE DYAD FORMAT

The main technique practiced on the intensive as mentioned earlier is called the dyad: a structured form of partner-assisted meditation in which two people sit across from one another to contemplate and communicate. Each participant first selects and focuses on one of five fundamental questions during the retreat:

Who am I? What am I? What is Life? What is Another? What is Love?

Ten to twelve times a day participants choose a different partner and sit across from one another on a pillow or a chair that is a comfortable distance apart. During each 40-minute dyad, the two partners take 5-minute turns being the contemplator/communicator or the attentive listener. The instructions are simple: set about to experience directly the essential Truth underlying the question and then tell the partner whatever occurs. There is a rest, walk, lecture, stretching or meal after each dyad.

This is all done in a supportive environment under the guidance of an experienced facilitator and staff. No religious or philosophic belief system is taught. The workshop leader is only a facilitator. He/she does not tell participants what to believe and only gives instructions on the technique to guide individuals through any difficulties that occur as they do it.

THE GUIDELINES

During an Enlightenment Intensive retreat, participants are asked to honor a number of guidelines. These agreements support the emotional safety, focus and effectiveness of the retreat. Participants agree to:

- Eat, sleep and stay at the site during the Intensive.
- Keep confidential anything that is said by others.
- Refrain from evaluating fellow participants.
- Take care of all outside concerns before the Intensive and allow any non-essential messages to be handled by the retreat staff, except for emergencies.

- Eat only the food and snacks served.
- Avoid smoking, illegal drugs, alcohol, or caffeinated beverages. (It is suggested to limit these a week prior to the retreat to avoid withdrawal symptoms.)
- Leave adornments such as jewelry, makeup, perfume, cologne, and other scented products at home or in the car. Non-scented deodorant is acceptable.
- Keep at home or in the car anything that may become a distraction such as books, magazines, journals, radio or tape/CD player, cellular phone or laptop.
- Refrain from all sexual activity.
- Put aside all other practices and put all efforts into using only the techniques taught during the intensive.
- Observe silence outside the dyad sessions.

THE SCHEDULE

The schedule is similar but not exactly the same as many typical meditation retreats. Participants begin the day on Friday, Saturday and Sunday at 6 am and go until approximately 10 pm with an hour of rest in the afternoon. The day is structured with dyads interspersed with meals, snacks, outside walks, exercise, talks and silent sitting.

IS IT REALLY POSSIBLE TO GET ENLIGHTENED IN 1 ½ TO 4 DAYS?

One of the biggest barriers to awakening (and people attending the retreat) is the belief that awakening cannot occur in 1 ½ to 4 days, that it must take a lot longer. This may be the case in other traditional forms of meditation but not the case with the Enlightenment Intensive. In the 50 years since Enlightenment Intensives began, there is confirmation from thousands of people all over the world that

147

the same experience that people have attained using other forms of self-inquiry or meditation taking from two weeks to 10 years, occurs on the intensive in only 1-½—4 days. A significant percentage of participants succeed in this time. Experienced truth seekers who have found difficulty in the past with other methods may find all their previous attempts rewarded during this concentrated effort.

Those new to self-inquiry often find it easier than veteran seekers who may have to overcome their own expectations and preconceived ideas of what the awakening experience is. And many report having Enlightenment experiences on the way home or in the days or weeks following the Intensive.

THE STEPS LEADING TO ENLIGHTENMENT

There are eight steps or stages that people pass through during the Enlightenment Intensive retreat on the way to having a direct experience of the Truth. Participants may go through some or all of these stages or they may spend a lot or a little time in each stage and return to previous stages or jump ahead a stage.

1. Giving Answers
One gives their partner answers that are already known. These have been learned from parents, teachers, clergy and friends. They may have been acquired in books or from other teachers. By presenting these answers to partners they are cleared from the mind.

2. Intellectualizing
One thinks things out logically and reasonably, e.g. "If this is true, then that must be true" and so on. Sometimes in this stage one may come upon the so-called correct answer. But answers correct or not, are not what one is looking for. This stage is finished when one stops trying to answer a question and begins to set about to experience reality directly.

3. Phenomena

One may have been overusing the brain to such a degree that it may begin to produce unfamiliar mental and physical phenomena. Visions may appear. The room may appear to distort. One may see auras around people and things. One may experience hot and cold flashes or waves of emotion running through the body. Not everyone experiences these but once the phenomena are communicated to a listening partner in the dyad, they disappear.

4. The Void

One may find the field of consciousness empty. No thoughts occur and no progress appears to be made. At this stage one stops trying to make the Enlightenment experience happen by looking for the Self and instead allows the direct experience to occur with greater openness.

The difference between looking for something and allowing Enlightenment to happen may seem subtle but it makes all the difference in the world. This stage is also known as the quieted mind and is often the end goal of many schools of meditation.

5. Emotions

One may experience feelings of fear, anger, grief, sadness, apathy or the opposite, bliss and serenity, as one experiences and communicates the emotional sense of self, which has been confused with the True Self. Feelings of fear may arise when one de-identifies or separates the True Self from these mental-emotional ego states. The key to moving through these barriers is one's willingness to communicate these feelings and experience whatever it takes to find the Truth.

6. The Enlightenment Experience

Two things occur simultaneously. One will have a direct, conscious experience of Self while experiencing a release of energy. The direct experience occurs in a timeless instant and will be known as a definite breakthrough. There will be no doubt. One may cry in gratitude, experience ecstasy or laugh uproariously at the obviousness of the truth.

7. The Glow

The energy that has been trapped by holding onto the false sense of self will get released and one's presence will radiate as one stays in union with the True Self. This will continue until the direct experience has been fully presented to others.

8. The Pure Steady State

Once the energy is discharged and one spends time fully communicating the direct experience to partners, one will move into a steady state of being present in the True Self and be in contact with it directly. The steady state will continue into life to the degree that one continues to present their True Self to others.

THE VALUE OF ENLIGHTENMENT IN LIFE

We can take any workshop on success psychology, on how to be more effective in achieving and manifesting our goals and to a certain degree we will be happy, but if we do not know who it is that has succeeded we will have failed at being fulfilled in life. We will have become a successful failure. History is full of highly successful people who at the end of their lives have sadly grieved because they did not find true happiness. The tragedy is not that they died but that they did not truly live. They may have certainly reached all their goals but may not have fully engaged in life because they did not know what life really was and therefore did not fully engage in it. They may not have fully lived in life because they did not know who it was that wanted to live. They missed the point of life while some other personality was living their lives!

Similarly, many of us live in accordance to what we think life is and who we think we are. The important point is . . . we only <u>think</u>

we know. We are living from an intellectual concept that has been programmed over time by the family and culture in which we grew up. It is as if we are all actors born and raised on a stage, taking our cues and roles from all the older actors. We gain acceptance by our behaviour from others and think this acceptance verifies that our self-image is who we are. It is not. It is just a reinforced socialized personality. We are unconsciously stuck in it, thinking that others' ideas of who we are, is actually who we are. We suffer out of our own unconsciousness, not really knowing why we suffer.

When we live from a personality, we live in a reduced state of experience. The personality is, in reality, a false identity state that is created from a belief about ourselves and life and others: "I am no good", "I am unlovable", "I don't exist", "I am not important" or "Life is too hard", "You can't trust others", "Love hurts". Every experience we have is filtered through this personality and accepts or rejects the life experience that reinforces or does not reinforce the belief. We only see what we believe and we reject the rest. The false belief is, in reality, superimposed over us and we act according to this belief and continue to re-create the same suffering.

There are thousands of seminars and techniques that propose that the remedy to all of this is to just change your beliefs. "Change your beliefs and change your life", i.e. to affirm, declare or even implant in the subconscious through various forms of therapy a positive belief. But this is just like changing around the furniture on the deck of *The Titanic*. It is superimposing another personality over the Self. It is still a mask.

So to live from a personality means that the energy of life is buffered, that existence is experienced selectively only from a point view, and that we live in a prison bounded by the walls of our egos. Living from a personality will give some degree of happiness but we won't find true fulfillment in it. However, if we directly experience who we are, the one that is behind the personality and in fact the one who created our personalities, the possibility of greater fulfillment in life exists.

The potential is that we can become more engaged in life. We are more available to all experiences. We will experience joy more fully and also sadness more fully. We will laugh more and more deeply and when it is appropriate to cry we will cry more deeply. We will allow our experiences in life to flow through us and complete them rather than block them, deny them or suspend them because of the filtering quality of our egos. We can feel more in the flow of our lives.

We can have more rewarding relationships because we will be more available to others. Relationships are all about the authenticity of the connection. To truly have a satisfying intimate relationship it is essential that we know who we and what others are. If we do not know who we are connecting from and what we are connecting to, we will only connect to others through the buffer of a false personality. Trying to navigate through the maze of two personalities to truly touch one another when we are not self-realized is impossible.

Because we are more engaged in life, we can take any growth technique or religious practice and make more rapid and on-going progress with it because we can bring to bear our own personal power of choice to be open and grow. In the success area of life, we can make real progress towards real goals and actually be happy, because it is now the real self living in life.

It can turn a person on to Truth and the actuality of that Truth in day-to-day life. We can discover that there is more to life than just gratifying the senses; that this whole business of life is not just some random occurrence with no direction or purpose. We can make these discoveries not as ideas but as living facts. Such discoveries fundamentally alter one's life.

When we realize that fundamentally we all want to be seen for who we truly are and relate to others authentically, we will understand that just on a daily basis, living from our essential selves in real contact with others actually uplifts others through the natural dynamic of Co-evolution. As a side effect, people on the intensive gain communication skills by practicing the co-evolution technique almost without realizing it. Lack of real communication and real listening without evaluation or interruption causes the greatest suffering in life. On an Enlightenment Intensive they can make significant gains in this ability just by participating in the retreat.

In the end however, the retreat has only one purpose: Enlightenment. It is its own value because it is the fulfillment of life. That union with Truth, no matter how brief, is our inherent purpose and fulfilling that purpose is the greatest benefit gained from an Enlightenment experience.

> *"In short, the Enlightenment Intensive is a powerful method, which produces remarkably consistent results. The method has been developed thoroughly, tested all over the world, and participated in by thousands and thousands of people. It is the most effective method for self-discovery that I have ever seen, and it is one that can be used by almost anyone.*
>
> *It is an amazing development in the field of spiritual growth, to have the awakening project be available to such a large portion of the people in such an accelerated fashion."*
> —Charles Berner—originator of the
> Enlightenment Intensive.

A LIST OF BENEFITS

After an Enlightenment Intensive, participants commonly report feeling:

- More authentic
- Peace, contentment and lightness permeating their body
- Totally embodied as if they have finally come home to themselves
- Loving-kindness towards themselves and others
- Greater self-acceptance

- Psychologically whole
- More inner strength and inner resolve
- Freer to express themselves around others
- Improved intuitive ability
- Enhanced and balanced energy levels

Participants also report having greater capacity to:
- Be open and authentic in relationships
- Persist and accomplish personal goals
- Face and overcome problems and difficulties
- Fully experience love, joy and happiness
- Understand the deeper truths in traditional philosophy and religion
- Naturally and honestly be themselves in relationships
- Be assertive and communicate their needs
- Find meaning, inspiration and insight
- Make rapid progress in their personal and spiritual growth

WHAT FORMER PARTICIPANTS HAVE SAID ABOUT ENLIGHTENMENT INTENSIVES

"Enlightenment Intensives are very pure and powerful. The value they had for me I can't say enough about. Enlightenment made apparent to me what my mind is and what I am and I became conscious of what others actually are. As a result, my approach to Martial Arts completely transformed and my ability improved dramatically. I highly recommend Enlightenment Intensives to anyone."
—Peter Ralston—California, First non-Asian ever to win a World Championship Tournament of Martial Arts (1978 Republic of China)

"When I am in union with myself, sounds are as if inside my body, voices vibrate in my chest, colors are bright and

*clear, my love comes out without holding back; I speak
the truth clearly from deep inside me—totally satisfying
and pleasurable. My face and eyes look straight at others;
I am relaxed. Nothing in me wants to hide. There is no
judgment, of others or myself. My breath flows clearly as if
to my toes with no congestion, because there is no congestion
in my mind—because there is no mind.*

*I occupy every part of my body—nothing can hurt me.
I feel complete, wanting for nothing. I am gentle, at one
with others. I could not hurt them. I know their thoughts.
I do not think to do anything; it is done. There is no space,
no delay between my actions and me. I am appropriate,
balanced. Ecstasy flows through my body and being like
waves. I feel humble, grateful for this state of grace. The
truth has set me free . . ."*

—Osha Reader, Director of Origin
Retreat Center, California

*". . . Over and over I am asked, 'Tell me who you are'. Each
time . . . I turn inward and focus my intent on directly
experiencing the 'I am'" that is beyond thought, word and
action. Letting go of what I anticipate the experience to be,
my body begins to move. My back arches on an inhale, my
shoulders are thrown back and my face turns up toward the
sky with a long sigh that builds to a low moan on the exhale.
My muscles tense and relax in an undulating rhythm. Each
time I go into myself, the movement is more intense, my
breath deeper and faster. I had expected some kind of serene
peace or sense of all-encompassing benevolence, an infinite
stillness—not this heat, this surge of power, this explosion
of sensation and movement in my body. Gradually I stop
worrying about what others might think and open more
and more to the direct experience.*

*It's like riding a dragon through the night sky. I feel
the fire that is myself and more than me, and I ride the
flame. The boundaries between myself and the walls of
the room, the floor beneath me, the person across from me,*

the trees outside dissolve in the heat. All the edges are ash. There is nothing that is not dragon-winged with feathers of turquoise, vermillion, azure. For a moment I am afraid it will tear me open—and it does—and I am the dragon. The joy of no separation fills me, even as the heat continues to sear through me. I am the heat and the searing. Metaphor can only approximate what is beyond words. When I emerged from the Enlightenment Intensive . . . all of my worries about the future and my resentments about past hurts seemed, in that moment, very small when compared to the vastness that is both what I am and the reality in which I participate."

—Oriah Mountain Dreamer writing of her experience from *THE INVITATION* by Oriah Mountain Dreamer. (c) 1999 published by HarperONE San Francisco. All rights reserved. Edited and presented with permission of the author.

<u>www.oriah.org</u>

"I have found the practice of the Enlightenment Intensive to be an invaluable experience along the journey of discovery. I more or less stumbled on my first one, not really knowing what I was getting myself into. However, it has had a lasting effect on my daily life. I feel a greater sense of confidence, equanimity and, surprisingly . . . wonder. The methodology combines a form of Zen koan practice with Western relational psychology, though it is not aligned with any theoretical or philosophical school. The format is simple and demanding. To discover the truth of ourselves and of existence, we must necessarily move beyond the numerous and ingenious devices we employ to avoid its raw reality. For some people, the search for that truth is the only really meaningful activity of life. I would recommend the practice to anyone who falls into that category."

—Sandra Fiegehen, Ph.D.,
Psychologist, Peterborough

"*I recently attended my first Enlightenment Intensive in 2011. As a seasoned traveler of the Way, I can testify that the technique works. As time goes on, I find I'm only interested in what works: this does. During the retreat, my realization was a slow and gradual one—which was exactly my intention. What's more, as the weeks since the retreat have unfolded, I am delightfully surprised to discover that the retreat experience was only the beginning. My awakening process is very active and increasing in depth and clarity. I have happily added the dyad communication technique to my other practices creating a dynamite trio of practice. Thank you, Russell, for keeping this going and offering it to as many people as possible, as well as for your gentle guiding presence!*

—Pat Parisi, Counselor, Toronto

"*I've never in my entire 50 yrs been so happy and positive about my life. It's a totally different happiness than the one I used to know. It bubbles up from deep within and explodes through every cell of my body. It's totally awesome. I also, for the very first time in my life, don't worry about the constant approval of others about me. I KNOW WHO I AM and no matter what they say, this is ME and I'm totally happy with myself and who I am! This is such a breakthrough for me. I've had my downs as well since I left the Intensive but the downs don't even come close to the highs that I used to have. I have a totally new life! I'm totally out of the dark and dingy prison that I lived throughout all of my life. I've broken the shackles that I created and I feel totally free! Love and Compassion have a totally different meaning and feeling to me. I truly feel that I've got a second chance in life, and it couldn't be any greater and better. I feel so excited that I could burst!*"

—Eliane Priese, accounting,
Holland Centre, Ontario,

"I took my first E.I. in the early 80s, over 20 years ago and I am still reaping the rewards from that experience. I could not be the person I am today without it. So much so that I encouraged my partner to take last weekend's intensive and, although doubtful, she is now also amazed and has started blossoming like a brand new flower. I can't say enough about this system of reaching and discovering for the first time your own inner truths and discovering truly what a wondrous being you are. Your whole world will change before your eyes. So don't hesitate, GO for it. What you will get will be the real you, and you will love it".

—Rudi Colme, Artist/designer. Holland Centre

"After a day and a half at the seminar, on Saturday morning while I was eating breakfast, it happened. It was as if I had never been here before, I was born again, and everything was a brand new experience and what an experience it was. I then knew who I was. I knew that I was eternal.

It happened just like Russell said, I was eating breakfast on Saturday morning and, like the snap of the finger, I was awake, the light came on, and I knew who I was. Every thing was new, like I had never seen it before, and it was exquisite. I was born again, free to experience life with the knowing that I would never die. The body might go but I would live on."

—Roger Groulx, Ottawa, Ontario

"It (the E.I.) is truly a powerful technique . . . My, my, my. How does one find the words? The full realization of it (my Enlightenment) did not come until the second to last dyad on the third day. My question was . . . What Is Life? . . . Well . . . as I try to type the words, to share the experience, I feel myself holding back the words because no words can convey the Sacredness of it . . . LIFE IS THE FACE OF GOD . . .

These words have been parroted a million times by a million tongues but the truth is . . . And this is no

*metaphor . . . LIFE IS THE FACE OF GOD and I have
seen it. It is the very face which I have been searching for
my whole life and it is all-pervading, everywhere and ALL
There IS . . . There is nowhere I can be and nothing that I
can 'do', that is not BEING in the arms of The Beloved. This
very life that I am is that. To experience this is the Divine
Union of the Lover and the Beloved, which I have longed
for, my whole life, to experience. I did not know . . . I do
not know . . . whether I am Loving or being loved . . . That
was/is the predominate feeling coursing through me . . .
LIFE IS THE BELOVED, BEING and the UNION OF
IT is WHO I AM and it is so powerful.*

*At the moment of realization . . . the words of Rumi
shouted in my head. 'From the beginning of my life I have
been looking for your face but today I have seen it.'"*

—Kamakshi, Massage Therapist, Michigan

*"Had I not attended your EI back in the spring, I would not
now have the unshakeable strength of knowing deeply who
and what I am which sustains me on a moment to moment
basis in a quiet, steadfast, joyful way. I don't know why nor
can I explain it but I continue to wake up happy every day,
thankful every day and smiling at work even though I'm in
an impossible situation. Now that can only come from the
direct experience I had at your EI and without it I'm sure
I'd be discouraged, depressed, muddling through, cranky
and grousing like everyone around me. I have more energy
now than I've ever had in my life, my husband has been
unendingly and enormously supportive and understanding
and life is good. Tough, but good. Sometimes life has to
slam me up against the wall and let me deal with it so I can
discover more of who I really am. So, thank you, Russell,
for helping me to see the reality and beauty of life, how I
am not separate from all life but am one with all of life and
how the Universe supports us on so many levels in so many
subtle and very palpable ways."*

—Gail Buss, Philadelphia, USA

"I really had no idea what to expect when I went to the 'Enlightenment Intensive'. But it was rewarding beyond belief! By the third day, I was sitting in meditation contemplating the question, 'Tell me who you actually are'. I began to notice a strange sensation in the middle of my chest. It was like shutters were trying to open. There was an energy pushing them open from the inside but outside forces kept slamming them shut. But this energy was persistent. It was from my heart. Suddenly the shutters opened wide and stayed open. It was in that instant that I met my spirit. I saw that everything about me was divinely beautiful and infinitely perfect. I knew that I had always been and would carry on through infinity. I had an image of myself dribbling a basketball and going for a layup on the court. I had no idea if I made the basket because that wasn't the point. The point was that I got to live my life with ME! I got to experience life as myself. Everything, no matter what it was, no matter how magnificent or horrible, was still worth experiencing because I was the one living it and I'm the most precious, miraculous, joyful energy to spend the rest of my life with! I get to be me!!!! And 'me' is exhilarating and sweet.

I walked up to the retreat guide in the middle of the meditation and I said: 'I have something I want to tell you. I think I have the answer to your question.' He made space for me to sit down and I looked into his eyes and said tremulously, 'I am me!' A tear began to roll down one of his cheeks and a smile spread across his face like a proud father who has just watched his child take his first steps. He nodded his head jubilantly and hugged me warmly. From that moment on I felt like I had been given a new life. Through the rest of the sessions, I was giddy and would frequently break into cartwheels and jump up and down shouting, 'I am me! I am me!!' During the outdoor walking meditations, I remember singing at the top of my lungs, 'I'm singing in the rain!' Even though it was February and we were in the middle of heavy snowfall, I felt like everything in life was there for me and it was all so beautiful.

> *The power of that self-discovery was enormous in my life and it has carried me through many struggles since. The place in my heart that was closed is now open and alive with the knowledge that I am me. There is no need for anything else. I am fulfilled with this gift. And I am thrilled to be me. I don't know how else I could have ever come to the understanding that I am this infinite, completely perfect spirit. There is nothing more beautiful in life than the recognition of who you actually are!"*
> —Cheryl Laird, Guelph, Ontario

Enlightenment Intensives are not an exclusive part of any organization, religious or otherwise. Some of them are conducted under different names with minor modifications. There is nothing to join and no one to follow. The facilitators of Enlightenment Intensive Retreats are not members of any particular organization, religious or otherwise. There are, however, teachers, groups and schools who have added the Enlightenment Intensive in whole or in part to their teachings and practices simply because the technique works. If you are interested in attending a retreat, there is a contact list of Enlightenment Intensive facilitators at the end of the book.

OUR JOURNEY SO FAR

So we have come a long way in our journey of No-Dogma Gurus. We explored the purpose of a spiritual path, what Truth is and how to experience it. We have looked at methods that don't get us to truth, the power of dogma to trap us, and understood what Insight and Awakening actually is. We have examined the characteristics of Enlightenment and how to live from that state. We have also investigated the difference between a "dogma" guru and a real spiritual teacher and looked at our responsibility to become a conscious seeker and how to manage dogma. We explored the basic Co-evolutionary structure of existence and learned how, by refining this process, we can come to deeper insight and even Enlightenment through the process of the Enlightenment Intensive. It has been a wonderful exploration together but it could end up being just another book sitting beside your bed gathering dust from another author presenting:

more dogma, interesting ideas and possibilities that made a bit of difference in your life but not a lot.

It could become the kind of book that years later you noticed on your bookshelf and recalled: "Hmm, Co-evolution. I can't quite remember what was in that book but I think it was an interesting idea."

MISSION POSSIBLE

Your Task should you Wish to Choose it
What if this book could make a big difference in your life? **What if you could by-pass dogma and become your own guru?** What if this book could bring you solidly into your own unique spirituality through deeper insights and even awakening experiences that transform your life? Remember at the beginning of this book I said not to believe anything I say until you, in your own experience, prove it to be so. Remember I said that at the end of the book, the final word will be yours? Now it's time for you to be the judge. Why not choose to find out if this whole business of Co-evolution is true? As with anything, that choice to grow in awareness begins with you. That choice began eons ago anyways, when we decided to become conscious of our divine nature, become separate gods and relate to each other in a co-evolutionary universe.

Try being in your life now with this new awareness and keep working on improving your communication skills so that you can achieve greater mutual understanding with others and in so doing evolve spiritually. Even better, choose to start up your own Co-evolution group. When you organize a Co-evolution group you create an oasis in life where people can be understood, accepted, authentic and compassionate with each other. It can be a refuge from a confusing world, where individuals who don't feel they fit in any religion or spiritual practice will find a community of liked-minded truth-seekers. Overtime, such a group can develop lasting satisfying friendships that bring the deep fulfillment to life that most people yearn for, in their hearts.

It is relatively easy to form a Co-evolution group. All you need is yourself, one other person and a set of procedures and instructions which I will provide in the next chapter.

CHAPTER 14

ORGANIZING A CO-EVOLUTION GROUP

It is relatively easy to form a co-evolution group doing dyads, as the group can consist of two or more people. Here are some suggestions:

Start off by scheduling a period of time of one to three hours to do one or two dyads. (Once you do one or two dyads, you can schedule in a day of dyads later if you wish). This could be in the evening or daytime. Invite people to attend and explain in advance the concept of co-evolution and how the dyad process works. Have chairs or cushions for enough people, a list of dyad instructions on paper Kleenex boxes, a timer that can be set for five-minute intervals, and some snacks/tea for after the session. If available, have one person who is experienced in doing dyads to explain the process.

PROCEDURE:

1. Start off the group with a brief sharing circle. Have people introduce themselves and say a little about what they are challenged with in their lives right now. (This can be

useful for them when selecting the instructions they want to work on).

2. Read over the guidelines for the group and ask everyone to agree to them. (See Guidelines below)

3. Read over or explain the procedure for doing dyads for any newcomers and answer any questions they have. (See Co-evolution Process with the Dyad technique below) Sometimes it is helpful for two people to demonstrate the technique briefly.

4. Have people assemble in the room in pairs sitting directly across (not at an angle) from one another. A good distance is to have chairs approximately 18" apart.

5. Pass out the dyad instruction sheets. Ask people to select a dyad to work on (some dyads have more than one instruction) and tell their partner which instructions they are selecting. Have people choose who will speak first.

6. When people are ready to begin say, "Listening partner give the instruction. Begin" and begin the timer so that it goes off every 5 minutes. Run the dyad for 40 minutes.

7. At the end of the 40 minutes each person should take one minute to share with their partner the most important thing they got from the dyad (without referring to anything their partner said)

8. Take a break for 10 minutes.

9. Repeat steps 5-7.

10. Have people sit in a circle at the end of the meeting and take one minute to share (without referring to anything anyone else said) the most important insight they got from the process.

11. Set-up the next meeting to remind people of the confidentiality agreement

12. Have snacks and beverages.

(* In the case where there are an odd number of people, the organizer can sit out and answer any questions that may occur as new people do the dyads or three people can do a triad where three people sit in a circle. In this case, two people are listening partners and the person to the right of the speaking partner gives the instruction to the speaker. At the end of 5 minutes, the speaker then gives the new speaker to his/her left the respective instruction(s) to the new speaking person. In a triad over a 40-minute period, two people will have three times to speak and one person will have two times to speak.)

GUIDELINES FOR THE CO-EVOLUTION GROUP

To establish a foundation on which open and authentic sharing can occur, attendees are required to agree to these guidelines for participation in the group. Group members agree to:

1. Keep confidential anything that another group member says or does during the duration of the meeting.
2. Avoid evaluating or communicating evaluations or judgments about anything a group member says or does during the meeting.
3. Touch or hug other members only after getting their consent.
4. Avoid commenting on or referring to anything any other group member shares during the Co-Evolution group.
5. Use "I" or "We" statements when sharing personal ideas and understandings, as the listener may perceive" you" statements as a personal comment or evaluation by the speaker.
6. Avoid giving advice to others.
7. Leave a donation to compensate for the costs of running the meeting if required.

8. Place any open beverage cups or glasses with liquid in it to the side of the room or on a table where it won't be accidentally knocked over.

A SUMMARY OF THE CO-EVOLUTION PROCESS WITH THE DYAD TECHNIQUE

The Dyad technique helps individuals find greater clarity and greater access to inner truth. It is based on the principle that awareness increases as the result of supportive and authentic relating between two individuals, i.e. Co-evolution.

There are two partners involved in the Dyad technique. One is the listener and the other is the speaker. Typically the two partners sit on chairs, directly across from one another, a comfortable distance apart.

The Listening Partner
The listener has three roles:

1) To give an instruction to the speaking partner.
2) To listen and understand.
3) To indicate when he/she has understood the speaker.

The listener is to find out from the speaking partner the instruction or instructions that he/she will be working on and then give that instruction with the sincere motivation to understand what the speaker is communicating. The instruction is to be asked in the "Tell me . . ." format, exactly as written in the supplied materials.

When the instruction is given, the listener is to make and maintain eye contact with the speaking partner and listen and understand without distracting or facilitating the partner's communication in any way. This means one must try to avoid nodding, smiling, making any verbal or non-verbal gestures of agreement or disagreement, or touching the partner. The listener is to avoid engaging in a conversation with the speaker or trying to encourage more sharing by the speaker. This will provide an opportunity for the speaker to take the time he/she requires to contemplate the subject without the distracting influence of the other partner. The partner is to keep confidential what is shared.

If the speaking partner says something that the listener does not understand, the listener can use the instruction: "Say that again" or "Summarize that". If the listener cannot hear the speaker, the listener can say: "Say that again louder". On rare occasions the listener may give the instruction "Clarify the term . . .", if the listener does not understand a terminology or concept that the speaker has presented.

When the listener has understood what the speaker has communicated, the listener is to indicate that he/she has understood by saying "Thank you". If the speaker has a 2- or 3-part question, the listener is to give the next part of the question and say "thank you" when he/she has understood. If the speaker completes working on his/her set of questions, the listener is to give the first instruction in that set again.

This process of giving an instruction and acknowledging with a "thank you" will continue for 5 minutes, until a timer bell sounds or until the session leader indicates to "change over".

When the bell sounds or the change over is indicated, the session leader will say "Thank your partner". The speaker will end the communication and the listener will say "Thank you". Another gong will sound and the leader will say "Change over". This will indicate a reversal in the roles as the listener now becomes the speaker and the speaker now becomes the listener who then gives the respective instruction to his/her partner.

The Speaking Partner

The speaker has 3 roles:

1) To receive an instruction from the listening partner.
2) To communicate a response that will be understood by the listener.
3) To avoid referring or commenting on anything his/her partner has said.

The speaker is to receive the question from the listener and contemplate the question silently. When the speaker comes up with a response to the question, he/she is to communicate it to the listener without adding or taking anything away from what he/she just came up with and in such a way that the listener will understand.

It is extremely important that the speaker not evaluate or refer to his/her partner or comment on anything that's been said. The speaker should use "I" statements (self-referencing) and avoid the use of "you" terminology as this could be interpreted as a reference to his/her partner.

When the listener has understood and says "thank you", the speaker will receive the next instruction in the series or receive the same question again if there is only one question he/she is working on.

If the listener says "Thank you" and the speaker is not finished getting across his/her communication and the gong has not sounded, the speaker is to continue communicating until he/she feels complete. This process of:

1) receiving the instruction
2) communicating the response, and
3) receiving the next instruction after the listening partner says "thank you", will continue until the gong timer or the session leader indicates the changeover.

Timing

The changeovers occur every 5 minutes. An introductory exercise for those learning the process normally lasts 20 minutes and the full Dyad technique usually lasts 40 minutes.

Benefits

Unlike solitary contemplation or meditation techniques, the Dyad technique is much quicker at producing insights and dissolving problems. The effect is the result of these 5 elements:

1) Agreements
2) Specific instructions
3) The listening partner
4) Silent inquiry
5) Communication

1. Agreements

The agreements of confidentiality, self-referencing, avoiding evaluation, facilitation and commenting on the partner's sharing are absolutely crucial to the process. Lack of these rules of engagement in life is the reason why we are all emotionally-injured and suppressed. These agreements form the container to allow individuals in their own time to feel safe to open up to their own inner landscape and to authentically present and be free of what is holding them back in life. It is valuable to have a facilitator or leader in the room to monitor the dyad session and offer corrections for beginners so that the two partners are not involved in complications that may arise from their own interventions.

2. Specific Instruction

Having an object of one's inquiry such as "Who am I?" or "What is my purpose?" gives the mind a focus rather than just putting one's attention on a candle or the breath and hoping that new understandings will occur. In addition, having the listener give an instruction versus a question has proven to be more effective. When the listener gives a clear instruction such as: "Tell me who you are?", he/she is directing the listener to do something and come up with a response and communicate it. The listener is instructing the person to be involved in the relating process. The question: "who are you?" does not necessarily imply a communication, whereas an instruction is more direct and engaging.

3. The Listening Partner
As the listening partner gives a very specific question to the speaking partner, he/she puts his/her attention on the listener. This is extremely helpful to the speaker. It is estimated that 50-80% of the time spent in typical solitary meditation practice is spent being distracted by extraneous thoughts and sensations. However, the presence of the listener awaiting a response keeps the speaker on track with less time wasted "spacing out" or losing touch with the object of contemplation.

4. Silent Inquiry
The presence of the listening partner has another function, very palpable to the person contemplating. The attention of the listening partner on the speaker gets added to the attention of the speaking partner during his/her silent contemplation on the subject. As they are both focused towards the same end, i.e. the speaker wanting to gain insight on the subject and the listening partner wanting to hear the result of the inquiry, the speaker is encouraged to take the contemplation deeper.

5. Communication
The communication that occurs after the silent contemplation has a clearing effect. It externalizes what the speaker came up with in the silent inquiry and as words are given to an often subtle or amorphous thought, feeling or sensation, the subject comes more into clarity and integrates into one's consciousness. With more communication,

understanding is increased. In addition, as internal thoughts, feelings and sensations are presented outwardly to another, the speaker is able to "let go" of suppressed inner states that he/she has been holding onto for years and years. The speaker can experience the exhilaration of an "aha" moment of deep insight and also the new energy and aliveness as he/she becomes liberated from an old emotional or mental pattern.

The Communication Cycle is probably the most significant benefit in this process.

It involves:

- The listener giving an instruction to the speaker and the speaker receiving it.
- The speaker looking within and contemplating the object of their inquiry.
- The speaker communicating to the listener exactly what they came up with in the contemplation.
- The listener acknowledging that he/she has understood.

The assumption behind the Dyad technique is that the mind is composed of incompleteness, i.e. the suspension of communications and experiences that an individual was not fully able, in the past, to get across to another. As an individual communicates these thoughts and feelings to another individual, in the safety of the Dyad process, and the receiving person understands them, the Communication Cycle is completed. The associated confusion, trauma and erroneous beliefs disappear and the mind gets clear. The truth that was obscured in the incompleteness is seen and spontaneous realizations related to problems or even awakening can occur.

Conclusion

The Dyad technique in many ways combines the ancient Eastern practice of contemplative meditation and adds the western method of relating (drawn from modern psychology). The synthesis of both results in a method that is a vast improvement over each one individually. When ultimate questions such as "Tell me who you are" or "Tell me what life is" are utilized, insights can occur quickly and awakening can even occur in 2-5 days. It is estimated that the dyad technique is 50-100 times faster at producing Enlightenment experiences compared to many traditional forms of meditation. As such, this method is particularly suited to our faster-paced, results-oriented western culture. The process of co-evolution of consciousness that is naturally occurring already in life, but impaired by the lack of safe rules of engagement is vastly accelerated.

Just as technology has advanced, so too has self-actualization technology. The Dyad technique is an outstanding example of this, establishing itself as a revolutionary awareness tool in the modern era of Human Development.

CHAPTER 15

SUGGESTED
CO-EVOLUTION DYADS

I have included in this book a number of my favourite dyads with the theory behind the wording and instructions on how to do the Dyads. In addition, I have also included a number of dyads under different subjects of inquiry that you can try out.

SELF-ACKNOWLEDGEMENT AND SELF-IMAGE

It is quite common for those on a path of personal unfoldment to focus excessively on aspects of themselves that need improvement, that are incomplete and need healing while ignoring the progress and accomplishments they have made in the past.

This tendency can draw us, over time, into a belief that we are perpetually incomplete, broken and are therefore condemned to a viscous cycle of constantly trying to fix ourselves. This is often the trap of perfectionism, the endless pursuit of never getting to there . . . of never being satisfied with being okay in the present and believing in only future happiness. Part of this disposition is the attention on what is wrong rather than seeing what is true and good about us. If we cannot see the goodness in ourselves, then we cannot let good things happen to us in life because we feel undeserving.

An aspect of this pattern is overlooking what is, in fact, true about us underneath what others consider to be undesirable. If we cannot acknowledge what is true about ourselves then we will be very susceptible to the opinions of others and feel weak in our own self-image. What makes us strong in our self-image and resistant to the negative views of others is the self-recognition of what is good, honourable and well-meaning in ourselves. Often the best way to get in touch with what is true is to contrast it with what is not true. As we get clearer on what is not true, we become clearer about what is true.

Being trapped in a negative self-image also causes us to deny the successes and achievements we have made in life, relegating us to a path of constant effort with hard-won results. We may actually have many successes but because we are not recognizing and being happy with them, we can feel like a failure.

In reality, success is a series of steps of smaller accomplishments not just a one-time achievement. We take a small step towards a goal, complete it and then take another step, complete it and soon the larger goal is reached. In order for us to continue being successful, we have to enjoy when we have attained each smaller goal. If we don't let in or emotionally receive each smaller success, this can block further progress because, in actuality, the final step in any small achievement is the enjoyment of that final step of attainment. If we don't acknowledge the completion of these intermediary steps, we may feel that these steps were incomplete, making the next step more difficult to take. Part of the problem is due to our being socialized to not brag about ourselves. We are told we should not be egotistical, or if we fully enjoy our successes in life then disaster is just around the bend. As the stoics of our culture impute: "Happiness will only be taken away if we enjoy it too much."

These Dyads can help dissolve these barriers and bring about a positive self-image based on our real successes, good intentions and genuine acts of concern for others rather than pumping ourselves up with fluffy new-age aphorisms that someone else has created for us to repeat.

If you are new to the co-evolution process, these Dyads are great to start with. The key to the effectiveness of these Dyads is to allow ourselves to go ahead and brag about our accomplishments and good acts. Choose one of A, B, C, or D and do each for 40 minutes (5 minutes each way) before going onto another set.

Self-Acknowledgement Dyads

A.
Tell me something you have accomplished in life?
Thank you
Tell me how this has helped you and others?
Thank you

B.
Tell me something that is true about you.
Thank you
Tell me something that is not true.
Thank you

C.
Get the idea that you are okay as you are and tell me your comments
Thank you
Get the idea you need to be perfect and tell me your comments
Thank you

D.
Tell me something you have done that was good for yourself or others in your estimation.
Thank you

Tell me something you avoided doing that was good for yourself or others in your estimation.

Thank you

Tell me any comments you have.

Thank you

PROBLEMS

There's an old saying that there are two things in life of which you can be certain:

death and taxes. There is, however, another thing of which we can be sure: having problems. We are going to have problems that irritate us, no matter what we do. They are a part of life. Everyone has them and as much as we tend to put out the impression that we've got life together and we don't have problems, actually we all have them. Guaranteed. Since this is true, then it seems obvious that we should learn methods of solving them. There are certainly lots of methods that we have learned of solving problems in school, such as mathematical problems, mechanical problems, organizational problems, etc., but we have not been educated to solve personal problems.

This is the problem we have with problems. We often avoid them because we don't know how to solve them, thinking that the avoidance of them will make them go away. But they don't and often get worse as we resist them. So in this discourse we are going to learn a few basic problem-solving methods.

Let's first start-off by examining why problems exist.

Problems are "the result of a non-understanding or a misunderstanding of something in ourselves or between ourselves and others, and a perceived lack of ability to engage in the activity to solve the problem". For example, we may have a problem at work completing lucrative projects that we start. We begin with a lot of excitement and then the energy fades and we don't understand why this happens. Other people depend on us to get things done, we don't get the project finished, they get angry at us and they think we are doing this deliberately to sabotage them, and then we aren't talking to them. So in this situation something is going on inside that we don't understand, others do not comprehend it either and we feel we don't have the ability to talk to them about it. So we've got a big problem.

The main thing that keeps it all in place is a lacking of understanding.

There are aspects of the problem that we don't comprehend and, as a result, they are hidden so we don't have sufficient information to make a decision on what to do. In addition, parts of the problem may be hooked up to other elements in the mind that should not be hooked up. Everything is all balled up together in tight knots, one thing tied to another and another knot entwined with something else so that we cannot see all the elements separately. We may have the idea of money tied up with greed or the idea of telling the truth with hurting others.

So if we try to work on a solution without being fully aware of all the aspects of the difficulty, we can get into greater difficulty by trying to impose a solution that only works temporarily until the unknown parts of the problem re-engage and then drag us down again. So to effectively solve a problem, we should hold-off on trying to solve it right away and instead spend a lot of time, as it were, pulling it apart, examining it, and trying to understand all aspects of the problem. One can call this a diagnosis or an assessment.

So the first step is obvious: Face the problem. It won't go away if you don't face it.

The next step is to totally understand every aspect of the dilemma. We should communicate to another everything about the problem so that we (and the other) can understand it completely. We should not worry about being coherent or organized. We should just state it however it comes out. Let whatever emotion or upset be there as well. Let everything come out. Let ourselves discharge. Often the blocked emotions are covering up seeing what is really going in inside. Once this is done, we can then go to the third step: to summarize the problem as we see it in the new present moment. Once we have taken it all apart we re-assemble it again. We put it into a one—or two-sentence re-statements. We gather up everything we have said into its essence and communicate it in the Dyad to the other.

The fourth step is to continue expanding and contracting the problem as in steps 2 and 3 until we have an epiphany, such as "Aha, this is what the problem really is all about." Often the solution is hidden in the problem and when the essence of the problem is clear, the solution will stare us in the face. With it will appear the awareness of the right actions to take. "Well, the reason I don't complete my projects is I am afraid that people will like me if I do a good job and underneath the face I present to the world, I feel I am no good. I find it uncomfortable when people like me. What I need to do is have people understand what I am going through and just go ahead and allow myself to be liked!"

Another alternative method to solving problems is to understand the general structure of problems, how they are put together or constructed and then breakdown the problem into this structure.

If we examine any personal problem, we will eventually notice that it has a basic simple structure of a goal and a barrier. Anytime we want something and there is something in the way of achieving it and we don't know how to achieve what we want, we have a problem. This is fairly obvious once we look at all problems. If we have an outcome that we want to achieve and there is nothing stopping us, then we achieve it. If we don't have a problem or if we have a goal and we decide we don't want it anymore, we wouldn't have a problem (e.g. "Well I wanted to go to university and become a brain surgeon but I think I'd rather work at a grocery store so I don't have a problem any more"). But if we want something and try to get it and something stops us and we still want it, we've got a problem.

Sometimes the problem is also composed of two opposing goals. We would like to not work so much but in order to afford to not work so much, we have to make a lot of money and that means working.

Another way we could have a problem is having a goal where the barrier is just impossibility and the goal can't be accomplished. "Well I want to fly to the moon by flapping my arms." We could spend the rest of our life trying to do that but never succeed. Or another problem could be the barrier is just too big to overcome in our present state of ability. If we say we want to cut down a big old tree with a nail file, maybe we could do it in 110 years but the tree is just too big. The problem lies in the fact that we don't see the impossibility of what we want to do.

Often dividing up the problem into a goal and a barrier makes the energetic dynamic of it much clearer. Once it is clear, then we can perform steps 2, 3 and 4 above on the barrier and then go back to re-stating the goal and barrier anew until the problem and its solution become clear.

Problem Clearing Dyads

A.
Tell me everything about a problem you are having so that I can understand it completely.
Thank you
Summarize the problem as you see it now.
Thank you
(Repeat steps 1 and 2)

B.
Tell me a goal you have in life.
Thank you
Tell me what's stopping you from achieving this.
Thank you
Summarize the goal and barrier as you see it now.
Thank you

Tell me something you can do.

Thank you

(Repeat steps 1, 2, 3, and 4)

ACCEPTANCE

There is a modern saying in life: "Life is what happens while you are busy making other plans". Oftentimes we look back on life at how things turned out differently than we planned and, in many ways, things turned out better than we thought. In looking back at difficult circumstances, we realize these needed to occur because they made us stronger or certain events were required to happen as a precursor to better things happening. In looking back, we see an underlying wisdom to these events. It sometimes seems there was a guiding hand or a destiny behind them even though at the time we resisted and could not accept these circumstances.

This so-called guiding hand in some traditions might be called the Tao, or "the way of life". We might say it's the force of life or the energy of evolution.

What it is, is the reality of existence or the nature of consciousness. It is a motivating force of growth through us as we encounter others and relate to them through challenging circumstances. And through this relating, we co-evolve, we become more aware of our self, life and others.

But we can resist this evolution and consider it a threat. The change can undermine our basic sense of security especially when the change is difficult and out of our comfort zone. But when this evolutionary thrust presents itself, resisting it only causes us more pain. The force of evolution just builds up and up like a dam and eventually bursts into our lives through a crisis that forces us to grow. There may be a job that we hate or a relationship that is not working for us and we don't have the courage to take the leap out of a secure but painful situation. The force of life may jettison us out of the situation with an extreme turmoil that moves us out of our comfort zone.

One of the ways we can integrate this evolutionary change into our lives is to try to see the event from a different point of view than "this is a disaster". Once we interpret the circumstances from a different perspective and accept them as a new opportunity in our lives, we can actually take advantage of the new dynamic.

Acceptance Dyad
Get the idea of accepting a situation in your life that you cannot accept and tell me what you experience.
Thank you
Tell me a different point of view you could take towards this situation.
Thank you

INNOCENCE

One of the most profound insights is discovering the essential innocence of our true nature. We have been socialized since birth that we are somehow flawed, imperfect and even evil.

This programming (which I have referred to in another chapter as a form of mass hypnotism) originates primarily from our Christian heritage in the West but is certainly part of other religious traditions. We have been lead to believe that we were born in original sin and when we are given unmonitored free will, we will commit all kinds of harm to others and ourselves. This point of view leads us to the conclusion that we have to discipline our children and each other in such a way that we remove this tendency and extract this condition of inherent badness. Generations of parents stuck in this point of view have used all manner of punishment, shaming and abuse to beat out the perceived badness in their children.

Taking on this point of view leads us into all kinds of neurotic behaviour such as second-guessing ourselves, self-hatred, trying to be good but continually coming up short, inviting victimization as a way of self-punishment and holding out the richness of life. We are hoodwinked into thinking that we need someone else or some dogmatic belief system to save us from ourselves because we cannot trust looking within to follow our guidance. This creates a sense of disempowerment and life-long, lingering helplessness. Many groups, religious orders and even countries have used this point of view to justify imposing their sense of goodness on others, with the rationale that the end justifies their means because they know better and have a higher moral ground than the people they impose their will on. Many do-gooders have actually created more harm than good to others operating from this belief.

The solution to this is to cast this concept of original sin into the category of dogma, to suspend our belief in it, and then examine for ourselves its verity of whether we are inherently bad or good. This dyad will be helpful for us to explore our essential nature in the realm of innocence. It consists of contemplating innocence and its opposite so that we can come up with our own conclusion. As we go back and forth in our contemplation, we will eventually extract the truth from what is not true.

Innocence Dyads

A.
Get the idea that you are essentially innocent and tell me what you notice.
Thank you
Get the idea that you are essentially sinful and tell me what you notice.
Thank you

B.

Get the idea that you are inherently good and tell me what you notice.

Thank you

Get the idea that you are inherently bad and tell me what you notice.

Thank you

C.

Get the idea that you grow in awareness by relating to others and tell me what you notice.

Thank you

Get the idea that you do not grow in awareness by relating to others and tell me what you notice.

Thank you

THOUGHT CLARIFICATION

Often the worst kind of problem in our relationships is the problem of knowing we have a problem but not knowing what it is. We don't quite understand why we are not connecting. . Sometimes it comes down to the fact that we have a thought barrier. We communicate to others with terminology and concepts that they or we do not fully understand. Or we communicate to others with an understanding of concepts or terms that differ from another's understanding.

For instance, we may have a problem feeling successful because we do not understand what success actually means. When we do not understand what it is we are trying to accomplish, the likelihood of accomplishing it is slim. We may encounter problems in a close relationship because we may have a different understanding than our partners on what marriage is. If that is the case, we may be trying to create something that is different than our spouses and come into conflict as we try to force our definition on them.

This is far more of a problem than we realize. Often the difficulties we can have in any kind of relationship at work, in families, groups, institutions even on a broader international and political level, can be traced to something very simple: the differences in definitions of words. Often we argue and cannot come to an agreement because of a non-understanding or misunderstanding on a basic level in the meaning of the concepts and terminology that we are using.

If we suspect that semantics may be the problem with others, we should stop and establish a mutual understanding of some of the basic terminology that surrounds our discussion. A good simple question is this: "Tell me what you mean by_____" or even simpler "Clarify _____" and insert the term in the blank. Another option is to go to a dictionary and look up the word to see how it is commonly defined as a first step in creating an understanding.

The important point here is this, if we have determined that a disagreement in conceptual understanding has occurred, and then this has to be corrected. We should not go on in the discussion until a mutual understanding of the terminology is established. Mutual understanding means that both parties have the same definition.

Another method is called Thought Clarification where we extract what something is not from what it actually is. For instance: when gold is purified, the gold is melted and it goes through a process where the impurities (or what is other than gold) are removed so that all that is left is gold. It is pure, meaning: "nothing other than itself as itself". There is nothing other than gold mixed in with gold.

Thought Clarification works in a similar way by contemplating what a concept is in comparison to what it is not. As we differentiate anything from what it is not, we get clearer about what it actually is.

To do this, use the following exercise which is best done in a dyad format. Here are some examples of values and concepts to start with: competency, individuality, dogma, equality, integrity, responsibility, respect, loyalty, credibility, honesty, excellence, accountability, dignity, empathy, accomplishment, courage, wisdom, compassion, friendliness, discipline, generosity, persistence, dependability.

Thought Clarification Dyads

"Tell me what _____ is"
"Thank you"
"Tell me what _____ is not"
"Thank you"

Here are some suggested Thought Clarification dyads related to this book:

A.
Tell me what a spiritual path is.
Thank You
Tell me what a spiritual path is not.
Thank you

B.
Tell me what religion is.
Thank you
Tell me what religion is not.
Thank you

C.
Tel me what a guru is.
Thank you
Tell me what a guru is not.
Thank you

D.
Tell me what dogma is.
Thank you
Tell me what dogma is not.

Thank you

E.
Tell me how you can recognize dogma.
Thank you
Tell me a decision you can make.
Thank you

F.
Get the idea that your life is your spiritual path.
Thank you
Get the idea that your spiritual path is separate from your life.
Thank you

G.
Tell me what Truth is.
Thank you
Tell me what Falsehood is.
Thank you

H.
Tell me what knowledge is.
Thank you
Tell me what knowledge is not.
Thank you

BELIEFS

In a previous chapter, we explored how we form beliefs as result of trying to explain to ourselves the reason for an overwhelming experience in the past. These beliefs are often negative and self-sabotaging: "I'm no good", "Life is too hard", "Others are dangerous", and "Money is bad". As we discovered, once these beliefs are formed, they are triggered automatically and unconsciously when an experience or person similar to the past overwhelming incident appears in the present. We bring the past unresolved charge into the present, confounding and complicating the present problem, often making the current difficulty irresolvable.

Typical self-help techniques employ positive affirmations to overcome these negative beliefs but often they don't work. People with a weak self-image originating from emotional or physical abuse actually feel worse with affirmations. The positive statements only become a band-aid layered over the negative viewpoint and require constant repetition in order to work. The feel-good is only temporary and when the person slides back into the negative side, the failure to alter their state makes them feel worse.

These dyads operate differently than affirmations. Instead of trying to eliminate negative beliefs by replacing them with positives, these dyads work on rehabilitating our ability to deliberately be in opposite points of view by our own choice. In this technique, we start off picking a belief and then its opposite before the dyad begins and then having our partner insert the wording of the belief into the instruction. We are then given the instructions to move back and forth from one belief to the other. In addition, we are asked what we did to manufacture the belief. As we continue to do this, we experience that we are actually the conscious creator of the mental and emotional state and not the unwilling victim. This can get us permanently unstuck and freed from the belief.

Belief Clearing Dyads

Get the idea of believing _____ and tell me what you did to get that idea.

Thank you.

Get the idea of believing the opposite, _____, and tell me what you did to get that idea.

Thank you

Tell me any comments you have.

Thank you.

GUILT AND SHAME

Guilt is a common unconscious mechanism in life that can sabotage the best efforts of the finest souls in life. If you sense something is holding you back in life, have recurring bad luck, feel like a victim to the circumstances of life or others and just don't seem to get ahead in spite of your best efforts, you can suspect the mechanism of guilt is involved.

To overcome the influence of guilt, it is important to understand what guilt is, how it operates, the two types of guilt (neurotic and healthy) and how to clear it.

WHAT GUILT IS

Guilt is the feeling of remorse that arises when we make an error that hurts or adversely affects others or ourselves. It often is exacerbated by shame or self-hatred. When guilt becomes extreme we can get stuck in a dynamic of neurotic guilt that will hold back the good things in life.

NEUROTIC GUILT

Unhealthy guilt is based on a pay-back mechanism that operates in this manner: When we take an action that hurts another, we mistakenly conclude that the way out of guilt is to somehow pay back our error by self-punishment. We do this by restricting our opportunity to be in a similar situation again or hold back the good things in life until we feel we have paid back the debt we have created. For instance, if we have mistreated others with money, misspent it or robbed others, we think the solution is to prevent ourselves from having more money or let it slip through our grasp as a way of preventing further hurt. The underlying error is that we don't trust ourselves to treat others well in regards to money.

The problem with this solution is that the pay-back time is usually far more severe and longer than the original transgression. In addition, we add self-shaming into the mix, diminishing our self worth by negative conclusions such as "I am no good", "I am bad", "I am worthless", mistakenly thinking that we'll pay up the debt by putting ourselves down. This is only a false solution that creates more problems. As we get stuck in the attitude of "I am bad", the only behaviour that emerges from this state is self-destructive. The ensuing actions only reinforce the self-conclusion of "I am bad", which imprisons us in a vicious cycle of self-shaming, self-deprecation, bad action and being right about being wrong.

THE WAY OUT OF GUILT

The first thing to understand about guilt is that shaming ourselves is illogical. The reason is that in our basic nature we are good. You see, it is only because we are good in our hearts that we feel bad about the bad things we've done. If we were inherently bad, we would not feel bad about the bad things we've done. We would feel indifferent. We would not care either way.

In reality, we feel bad because we are good at heart. It is self-evident in the way that we feel when we do something we consider to be bad. Therefore to shame ourselves is inconsistent with our true nature.

Fortunately, there is a healthy way out of guilt. The way is to become conscious of our mistakes, to learn from them and contact our inner standard to guide us to make better choices in similar situations in the future. As we do this, we develop the confidence and trust that we will behave more ethically and honestly. We will then know that we will be less likely to make the same mistakes again and allow good things into our lives.

THE PROCESS OF GUILT CLEARING

There is a process that involves dyad work that, if followed, can significantly relieve us of unhealthy guilt and naturally bring good things into life.

1. Understand the Two Categories of Guilt

There are errors of commission and errors of omission, i.e. actions that we did and actions that we did not do about which we feel bad. When referring to guilt, we may assume this is related only to actions we committed. But guilt can also be related to actions that we could have taken but did not take, i.e. the failure to do something. For example: "I saw the person drowning and I could have jumped in the water and rescued her but I didn't."

2. Acknowledge

One of the most powerful things we can do in the process of releasing guilt is to simply acknowledge the naked fact of our mistake . . . to just say the main thing with no embellishment, e.g. "What I did was yelled and screamed at my innocent child", without any justification or story telling.

Often we can sidestep the impact of our transgression by justifying our action. "Well, he had been ripping people off in his business for years so I was just giving him a taste of his own medicine by robbing him" or we can dilute the impact of our actions by telling a long story about it: "Well it all started way back in '89 when she looked at me in an odd way and I kind of wondered what she was thinking and then in '91 she . . ." All of this just waters down our feeling of guilt. We should just look at the main event, the simple fact of what we did or did not do.

Even more powerful is creating a dyad where we can confess to another person what we did. It is important that the listening person just hear what we have to say without judging or giving advice on what to do. When we are done, the person acknowledges with a simple: "Thank you". There is a great release in just telling the truth. We can also confess it to God, a Higher Power, the Great Spirit, the universe or whatever represents to us some higher form of wisdom. What is important is to get this communication from the inside to the outside for a release to occur.

It is also important to say what we did or did not do in our own estimation. When we use someone else's standard, for example that of the law or the church, it can be a subtle way of avoiding taking responsibility. "Well it really wasn't that bad because I do not agree with what the church dictates." It needs to be an error that we judge to be hurtful in our estimation, according to what is in our own heart. By doing this we are developing our own standards of conduct and bringing our hearts into alignment with others.

3. Feel Guilty

This appears to be counter-instructive to what was just said above about feeling bad. Even though we are good in our nature, we should allow ourselves to feel bad about our transgressions but without the shaming. Why? Because when we allow ourselves to feel bad, we break through the barrier of denial. "Well I hit him because he looked like he was judging me and yes he was bloody but it didn't really hurt him that much." On the other side of this barrier is the stark truth of the transgression that was made. It is the acknowledgement of the full truth of our errors and the feeling of the remorse that motivates us to learn from our mistakes and change our future behaviour.

4. Retro-inspect

We should then look at what we could have done or not done differently. There is an old saying that hindsight is 20/20. In looking back at our errors and the effects of our actions on others and ourselves, we will distinguish more clearly what was right from what was wrong. In retrospection, we will learn from our mistakes and discover that in our hearts we really want to treat others well. This will give us confidence that we can make the right future decisions in similar situations. Knowing that we can create a different positive outcome allows us to let in good things in the future.

5. Learn

We should ask: "What have I learned from this?" Developing wisdom from our transgressions gives us even more trust that we can make the right decisions in the future. In the past, we held ourselves back from good things because we did not trust ourselves to make the right decisions about money, sex, power, love, etc. But the real problem was less about trusting ourselves and more about learning from our mistakes. When we know better, we will let our lives get better. We will trust ourselves to not abuse the good things in life and therefore allow more abundance in money, relationships, opportunities, etc. to flourish. So we must remedy this. The question: "What have I learned from this?" also brings us into alignment with the purpose of life. If the true purpose of life is the development of consciousness, then by inspecting what we have learned from our actions/inactions and acquiring self-knowledge from our mistakes, we move more into the natural flow of life.

6. Establish a Standard

The final step is to establish our standards. By learning from our mistakes we also access our intuitive ethical and moral guidelines which we can self-reference in any situation in the future: "I learned that other people have the same feelings as me and they get hurt in just the same way". There is an inner criterion here, a standard of treating others and bringing it to awareness. When we do this, it strengthens our moral character. We become more confident that we will act for the benefit of ourselves and others and allow goodness

193

into our lives. It turns out that our inner standard is very similar to the golden rule: "Treat others as you would have them treat you". But it is much deeper than this. It's connected to our true nature. We should treat others better because in our true nature we actually are others, so when we mistreat others we are actually causing harm to the whole fabric of our common unified existence. We harm our co-evolution together. On the other hand, because almost any progress in life is somehow associated with how we treat others, when we treat others better we become more successful.

In summary, by practicing these steps we can release our neurotic self-punishment, gain discrimination for future actions and move into greater harmony with the inherent co-evolutionary dynamic in life.

Here's an example of the steps:

"I took money from my boss by entering phony petty cash bills into his books and taking the money. What I would do differently is talk to him about my financial difficulties and either ask for a raise or an advance. I learned that when I am desperate for money that I should be honest and tell the truth first."

Guilt Clearing Dyads

We begin working through these instructions within the 5-minute period. Any instructions that we do not get through, we should ask in the next 5-minute period before beginning again on the first instruction.

A.
Tell me something you did that you think you should not have not done in your own estimation.
Thank you
Tell me what you would do differently, if you could, looking back on this.
Thank you

Tell me what you learned from this.

Thank you

Tell me something you failed to do that you think you should have done in your own estimation.

Thank you

Tell me what you would do differently, if you could, looking back on this.

Thank you

Tell me what you learned from this.

Thank you

B.

Tell me a standard you have for treating others better.

Thank you

Tell me a standard you have for treating yourself better.

Thank you

CRITICALNESS

There is a mechanism of the mind that can bring great suffering into working or family relationships. It's a mental activity that we secretly hide from others as the black secret of ourselves. Fortunately, this mechanism, when rightly understood and properly dealt with, can bring about mutual understanding, better relationship and a sense of connectedness to others.

This mechanism is called criticalness. We all have a sense of what it is. It is that automatic irritation we feel about others' behaviour. It is the silent mental putdown where we typify another as beneath us and less than human. It is that labeling of an individual as a jerk, idiot, phony, egotist, sexist, bitch, prude, nit-picker, airhead, etc. (You can add your own favourite names to the list). It is the compulsion within us to condemn and judge others.

In the play, *No Exit* by Jean Paul Sartre, a character complains that "Hell is other people." Deeply critical people take this point of view to the extent where they secretly dwell in a hell of condemnation in which others, not themselves, are the main problem in life. As they gradually push well-meaning people away, their lot in life becomes a state of loneliness and misery.

Being around individuals who condemn us can be very difficult. We feel we cannot fully be ourselves and have to constantly watch our actions. We hold back our true thoughts, suppress our feelings and resort to acting the way they want us to behave. But as we do this, unreality and emotional coldness enter the relationship and we find ourselves pulling away and establishing distance from them. We are compelled to do this as a natural, protective mechanism when we really would like to be open to them.

Unfortunately, modern television, through the proliferation of half-hour sitcoms, has elevated criticalness to the level of an art-form with the use of the one-liner put-down or the snide remark that effects canned laughter with an off-the-cuff underhanded insult.

But if we engage in this type of comic relating in our relationships, then life becomes a tragedy. Criticalness can contribute to people lashing out and emotionally injuring others over the most insignificant incidents. After the deed has been done, there's no laughter. People wonder what happened and feel deeply guilty about their behaviour. The parasitic legacy of criticalness is that it can kill any relationship, whether at work or at home.

Fortunately, there are steps to take to deal with criticalness in ourselves and others. I would like to introduce these to you now.

1. Acknowledge
The first step is to acknowledge the lack of value that criticalness has in your life. Ask yourself if you have honestly felt any better after entertaining negative judgments of others. Try this exercise:
Think a condemning thought of another person.
Notice how you feel.

Think a loving thought of another person.

Notice how you feel.

Then ask yourself: "Does criticalness make me feel any better? Has it honestly improved my life?"

Now ask yourself: "What is it like to be on the receiving end of another's belittlement? Does it uplift me?"

If you are truthful, you'll admit that criticalness has not made you any happier in life. In fact, I have never met a person who, after looking in their heart, said that they felt good about a working day spent being critical with others at coffee breaks and lunch. The first step is to acknowledge that condemnation of others has not enriched your life.

2. Choose

The second step is a natural outcome of the first: Make a decision to dissolve your criticalness. Choose to do something about it. Right here and now, make it a project to overcome criticalness in yourself. It may be true that you have been hurt by others' belittlement and you'd like to deal with this first. But if you are going to be successful at this project, concentrate in the beginning at handling your own criticalness. The more you understand where your judgments come from, the more you will understand the origin of them in others. In this way, you will be less affected by others' criticalness. In addition, the less you are irritated by others, the more likely others will treat you well.

3. Understand the origin

The fourth step to dissolving criticalness is to understand the origin of criticalness. If the source of our criticalness is not within others then where does it come from? One person aptly answered this question when they observed: "When you point your finger at another person you've got four others pointing back at yourself!" It is in us.

Carl Jung, the psychologist, has given some illumination on this. He discovered a mechanism in the mind which he called projection, whereby the individual takes aspects of his shadow side (the perceived negative, unintegrated side of one's unconsciousness) and projects or perceives this in others. Criticalness is related to this mechanism.

The reason that we become judgmental of others is because we see in others the things that we really do not want to acknowledge in ourselves. We project onto others the characteristics of ourselves that we have a hard time facing in our lives. So if I am critical of Harry for being a jerk, it's because in some way I have done something that's similar to him and I'm feeling uneasy about it. Others are actually mirrors of you without even trying to be.

The second reason that we get critical is related to misunderstanding. Where there is something not understood between two individuals, criticalness can arise. It occurs when, in your estimation, you think there is something that another person has not understood about you that you want them to understand and that you haven't fully communicated to them. Saying this in a different way, if I sense that another person hasn't received a communication about myself that I feel is important for him to understand, I'll get critical. But I'm responsible for this because I haven't gotten myself across to him. There may have been a number of reasons why he didn't understand: he didn't hear me, he was pre-occupied, he was distracted, he interrupted me or he just didn't want to hear me. Whatever the reason was, I didn't get across something about myself that I thought was important and I want him to understand what this is. It's up to me to get the person to listen and understand me.

Also of importance is to distinguish between being upset and criticalness. Criticalness is a mental state of finding fault in another and dwelling on it. Upset is different. Someone may not show up for an appointment after making a commitment to do so and I may get upset but I might not judge them for this. However, criticalness can often get enmeshed with upset and add more anger to the upset if I judge them negatively for this. (For example: "I'm angry at you for being late, you jerk").

4. Just Stop It

The fifth step in removing criticalness is: Stop expressing it. That's right. Just notice when you are finding fault in others and stop verbalizing it. Now this may seem like suppression, and in a way it is, but you will feel better for it. Because underneath our justification of our fault finding we know that we are participating in telling a lie. We know that in our hearts we are doing the best we can in life and we know it is so for others. So it is untrue that others are bad. In verbalizing our criticalness, we are also injuring others. Even though the person we judge is not there, we know we are poisoning another's point of view towards the person we are going on about. We feel guilty about this and as a way of compensating for our bad act we will keep good things out of our life and in turn attract verbal injury to ourselves.

5. Self-inspection

The sixth step in removing criticalness is to practice self-inspection. Whenever you notice yourself finding fault in others ask yourself: "What is it I am being critical of in others? What have I done that is similar to this?"

The key word here is similar. You may be critical of others because they lack control of their food consumption and what is similar in you is a lack of control in planning your business activities. Sometimes it takes awhile but when you hit the similarity, an amazing thing happens: your criticalness dissolves into nothingness. You become open to that person again and you have established a commonality with them ("Wow, they are working on the same thing I am working on!") You begin to have more compassion for them. In addition, you begin to be easier on yourself for your own faults as you notice that you are not alone in your imperfections. Sometimes, as a side effect, you will begin to seek to improve your own behaviour. Finally, you will naturally tend to treat others better out of real understanding of human nature.

Another thing you can do is ask yourself this question: "What is it that I feel is important about myself that I think another does not understand?"

When you are clear about this, communicate this to the other person so that you are talking about yourself without laying a trip on the other person. For example, there is a difference between these two communications:

"You make me angry every time you leave the toilet seat up, you idiot!" AND

"What you should know about me is that I like to keep the toilet seat down."

The first statement is putting down the other person and makes them responsible for your upset. The second statement is a simple communication about yourself that will lessen the tendency for others to get defensive and resist you. When your communication is complete, you will notice a remarkable dissolution in your criticalness and greater openness to the person in question.

You can also avoid participating in criticalness with others, or change the subject or just ignore it.

The problem of criticalness can gradually dissolve if it is taken on as a long-term project. These techniques are self-reinforcing, which means that simply by experiencing the moments when your fault-finding dissolves, and you feel freed from being critical, then you will tend to make these techniques automatic.

Criticalness Dissolution Dyads:
A.
Tell me what you are critical of in another.
Thank you
Tell me a way you are similar to this.
Thank you

B.
Tell me what is important about yourself that you think another does not understand.
Thank you
Tell me what you can do to bring about this understanding.
Thank you

LOVE

Love is one of the most beautiful emotions in the universe. Without love, life would feel flat and one-dimensional. We would not experience a connection to one another. Children would not be nurtured and be able to grow mentally and emotionally. We would not feel safe enough to expose our vulnerabilities to one another and release our pain and suffering. It is the glue that holds the universe together. It is the one infinite timeless catalyst that draws us all together so that we can relate and evolve.

The following dyads help us get in touch with love, expose the blocks we have to its experience and help us get out of our minds and into our hearts. Each section should be a 40-minute period.

Love Dyads

A.
Tell me what love is.
Thank you

B.
Be open to the presence of love and tell me what you experience.
Thank you

C.
Tell me how you want to be loved.

Thank you
Tell me how you want to love others.
Thank you

D.
Tell me a way that you have withheld love from others that was not best in your own estimation.
Thank you

ENLIGHTENMENT

The following questions are commonly used on Enlightenment Intensives. There is a difference between these questions and the insight questions. With these questions we are attempting to arrive at a direct experience of our object of inquiry, not a new intellectual comprehension. To understand the difference between an insight and direct experience, you can review the earlier chapter where this is discussed.

Our goal with these questions is to go beyond mental constructs, beliefs and concepts to an experience of the essential nature of Life, Self, Others, Love, etc. With these questions, the listener's guidelines are the same but you start off with a slightly different approach in your investigation. When you get the instruction from your partner, you need to start off with a real sense of the subject you are investigating, to make sure that you are not just dabbling around in theoretical musing. After receiving the instruction, you start off selecting a real experience of your object (life, self, another, love, etc.) that is occurring right in the moment. If you are inquiring into the nature of yourself, what is most real might be the pumping of your heart, the sensation of breathing or the discomfort of a back pain. If it is life, you pick a piece of life like a tree, a flower or sensation in your body that is palpably real in the moment. It is the same with the other questions. Then you hold that experience in your consciousness and place your attention on that object with the intention that you directly experience the essence of it. In the case of self, you want to become directly conscious of the one who is having the sensation of the heart beating or your breathing or a back pain. In the other questions, your goal is the same: to experience the true nature of life, another, love, etc. within that object and then we proceed to the next steps of being open and communicating to your partner. One question should be worked on for the 40-minute period.

These questions are qualitatively different than the insight questions. For the serious seekers of truth they are very compelling, drawing us into the deep mystery of existence and nourishing the deep yearning you have felt for the truth. One 40-minute period of dyading on one of these questions is not enough. But it can give you a taste of the power of the co-evolution process on these subjects. If you are seriously interested in awakening, you should enroll in an Enlightenment Intensive where you will be supported in moving through the stages of awakening that were described earlier in the chapter about the retreat.

Four fundamental Enlightenment Dyads

A.
Tell me who you are.
Thank you

B.
Tell me what you are.
Thank you

C.
Tell me what another is.
Thank you

D.
Tell me what life is.

Thank you

Alternative Dyads

A.
Tell me what love is.
Thank you

B.
Tell me what the mind is.
Thank you

C.
Tell me what consciousness is.

ENLIFENMENT

It is common after an awakening in any tradition for the openness to the new consciousness to last anywhere from two weeks to a few months before the expansiveness of the experience fades. You may still retain the knowingness of the truth but you can become disconnected from perceiving yourself or life from the new awareness. You know what you know and you know that you know but you may not be experiencing what you know. Someone who has been to a mountaintop and has seen the valley and the panoramic vista may still be in the exalted experience when they return to the valley but the feeling eventually subsides. What remains is the knowledge of the difference between being at the peak and living in the valley. Sometimes a spiritual depression can set in as the "high" of the awakening experience fades and one faces their ordinary life again.

The fading of direct experience is a result of the undissolved parts of the ego or mind gradually reforming around the Self and the lack of cultivation of the awakening experience. Let me explain this further.

You may have a direct experience or have realized a divine truth of yourself but there still is more knowledge to gain from that experience. You fall in love with someone but that's not the end of the relationship. It takes the rest of your life to get to know that person. There are barriers that come up in your relationship that need to be dissolved as you get closer to each other. It's the same with enlightenment. You have finally come home to yourself. You are in a new relationship with yourself. This is actually the beginning of the spiritual path! It is not the end! It's the start of a new life of being in truth when most of your self has been in illusion. I call this process Enlifenment, and it is enhanced with 4 processes: Clearing, Attention, Knowledge and Self-Remembrance.

Clearing

With Enlightenment, you have dislodged the foundation of your mind. Before enlightenment the basis of the mind was illusion, now it is the truth. Many of your dysfunctional ways of being, false solutions to life, traumas and limiting beliefs are still hanging around. They have metaphorically hit the fan and they are spattered all over the wall. They are still alive and kicking and will try to re-establish their sovereignty again. When they do, you will start to feel unbalanced and disoriented. You'll start to wonder "What the hell is going on. I thought I got enlightened. How come I'm feeling so unenlightened?" What has actually happened is that you have turned the light on in yourself so to speak, with your enlightenment experience. You are becoming aware of the conflicts within yourself that have always been there. Now you see and feel them. You are conscious of them.

You can run away from them, hide from them by adopting a phony spiritual personality or face them. It is now an opportunity to dissolve these so that you can be more fully in the radiance of your truth. Many of the solitary meditation spiritual practices (that may have gotten you enlightened) are a slow way to dissolve them. It is faster to engage in some short-term psychotherapy or energy work. The best forms are methods that are insight oriented, i.e. processes that, with the help of a skilled practitioner, bring you to your own understandings of how you have constructed your mind and ego and then assist you to dissolve them (see Clearing in the final chapter of the book).

Attention
If, after your awakening, you go right back into regular life and focus exclusively on the externals of existence—all the activities of your job, parental duties, watching TV, etc.—then the lack of attention to the awakening experience can cause it to fade. If you have not developed some strategy of how to live from this new awareness, particularly as you are relating to others, you can default into old patterns of relating and lose touch with the spiritual experience.

What you need to do is use your new awareness of yourself as your object of concentration in meditation. Instead of using your breath, a mantra, a picture, body sensation, etc. as your focus, use the truth of what you know as your focus. "I am just myself", "I am love", "I am everything". Start off your day connected to this awareness and come home to it at night. The more you place your attention on the truth of your being, the more you will be in yourself with your "doing-ness" in the world.

Knowledge
You have directly experienced the truth but there is still more to know. Maybe you have experienced that you are the ONE. You are the whole thing in the universe. You are IT! It's a big deal that's not such a big deal. It's a huge realization, but at the same time it's just the fact of existence. It's just the way things are, so what's the big deal? You should not stop there. There is more to know about you. For instance what are the characteristics of yourself? What are you composed of? What are your qualities—consciousness,

love, infinite potential, happiness? Get the idea? There's a huge list. So put your attention on yourself and then investigate the immense fullness that is within. The more you become aware of and differentiate all the different aspects of your true self, the more these come into balance .You will be more able to access these divine qualities in yourself and engage them in your relationships with others. When pure consciousness or divine love is part of your true nature, the more you will be able to relate to others with a clear mind and pure heart.

Self-remembrance

Many people on the path of consciousness feel that there is a separation between the spiritual and everyday life when in fact there is not. This separation is self-created. Everyday life is actually the testing and stabilizing ground for the spiritual experience, if the former two practices are used. The practice of Self-remembering is essential to bridging this gap. It is an extension of the Attention exercise. Whenever you are around or in a conversation with others, put your attention on yourself. Begin when you are a listener. Be in the space of your essential nature and then keep your attention on your self as you interact. Let the genuineness and open-heartedness flow from there. This, of course, will challenge you to stay centered in yourself. You will fall in and out of your connection as you begin this practice. But with more interaction with others, you will develop your ability to stay in touch with yourself. In this way you will begin to realize that life is not antagonistic to being who you really are. It is actually the optimal school of training you to "be-you-to-fullness" in your everyday relating to others.

With these ideas in mind here are some dyads designed for the purpose of helping you be more connected to your enlightenment as you navigate in the world.

Enlifenment Dyads

A.

Put your attention on a Direct Experience you have had and tell me what you notice.

Thank you.

B.

Tell me a difficulty you have presenting your true self to others.

Thank you

Tell me a decision you could make to live more from your true self.

Thank you

C.

Tell me a challenge you have with living from an awakening experience you've had.

Thank you

Tell me what you can do in your life to cultivate living more from this state.

Thank you

D.

Tell me what enlightenment is.

Thank you

Tell me what enlightenment is not.

Thank you

E.

Put your attention on your true self and tell me a quality of your true self.

Thank you

Let this quality expand in your awareness and tell me what you experience.

Thank you

Other Dyads that are valuable would be the ones on Authenticity.

CREATING YOUR OWN INSTRUCTION

There are obviously more aspects of Self, life and others into which we can inquire that are not covered in this book. I leave it up to you to create your own areas of inquiry based on your interest. Sometimes it can be a challenge to put a subject of investigation into an instruction, so here are some guidelines. Some ways of doing this are to discuss with your dyad partner an issue that has your attention in your life and brainstorm with her/him on an appropriate wording. In general, we should try to put the instruction into the "Tell me" form, with the "Tell me" at the beginning of the sentence and the verb at the end.

Sometimes you may be faced with an issue that you cannot fully articulate so a good question to start off with is: "Tell me something you are confused about" or "Tell me what you have a hard time describing".

Once you have given a response to the question, then have your partner put the subject into the form of: "Tell me everything about _____ (inserting the subject) so that I can understand it completely". Or "Tell me what it is about yourself in regards to _____ (inserting the subject) that you don't think others are understanding".

For example, you might say: "I have a hard time describing my feelings about a man I just met". You would then get your partner to give you the instruction: "Tell me everything about your feelings about the man you just met so that I can understand them completely".

Or it may become apparent that you can use an instruction in a different section, such as in the Thought or Belief Clearing section and you use this.

Some of the most powerful work can come out of being faced with an issue that you want to avoid. Here are some questions that you can have your partner ask you to get at these issues and begin to resolve them.

Dyads

A.
Tell me an issue that you find difficult to talk about.
Thank you

B.
Tell me a question that you do not want others to ask you.
Thank you

C.
Tell me something you find hard to face in yourself.
Thank you

For example, you might say in response to 1, 2 or 3. "Something I find hard to face in myself is an inability to face conflict in my relationship". You would then get your partner to give you the instruction:

"Tell me everything about your inability to face conflict in your relationship so that I can understand it completely".

Sometimes a "why" inquiry may come up in response to 1, 2, or 3. For example, in response to 2, you might say: "A question I don't want others to ask me is: 'Why do I let others take advantage of me'. Avoid getting your partner to ask a "why" question as this type of question can illicit an intellectual response or move a person into justifying or rationalizing their behaviour rather than understanding what it is underneath the behaviour that is causing it. A much better format is to word the instruction in terms of a barrier: "Tell me what stops you from asserting yourself around others" or "Tell me what it is in yourself that allows others to take advantage of you".

Creating your own instructions is a bit of an art but once you have done a number of the different dyads in this book, you will be able to do this. You may find that just varying the wording slightly can make a big difference in the effectiveness of the instruction penetrating right to the core of the issue. Experiment with this and have fun with it.

ADDITIONAL CO-EVOLUTION DYADS

Work on one section between the lines for the full time of the dyad (30-40 minutes)

Being Yourself
Tell me some concerns you have about being yourself around others.
Thank you
Tell me a decision you could make.
Thank you
Understanding
Tell me something about yourself that you think others have not been understanding.
Thank you
Tell me a decision you could make.
Thank you

Decide to be happy with yourself right now and tell me what you experience.
Thank you

Confusion

Tell me something in regards to _____ (insert topic) that you are not clear about.
Thank you
Tell me something in regards to _____ (insert topic) that you are clear about.
Thank you

Goals

Tell me a goal you have in your life.
Thank You
Tell me how you can be responsible to make this happen.
Thank you

Tell me something you think God wants for you.
Thank you
Tell me something you want for yourself.
Thank you

Success and the Law of Attraction

Tell me something you want to achieve in Life.
Thank you
Tell me a goal in this you believe you can achieve.
Thank you
Feel really good about achieving this and tell me what you experience.
Thank you

Completion

Tell me something you have not yet completed in your life.
Thank you
Tell me a decision you could make.
Thank you

Personal Values

Tell me what _____ is?

Thank You

Tell me what _____ is not?

Examples: competency, individuality, equality, integrity, responsibility, respect, loyalty, credibility, honesty, excellence, accountability, dignity, empathy, accomplishment, courage, wisdom, compassion, friendliness, discipline, generosity, persistence, dependability.

Self and Other (both partners work on the same questions)

Tell me what you are.

Thank you

Tell me what another is.

Thank you

Authenticity

Tell me the truth.

Thank you

Be here and now in your Real self and tell me what you notice.

Thank you

Tell me some concerns you have about being real around others.

Thank you

Tell me a decision you could make.

Thank you

Tell me something about yourself that you don't think others understand.

Thank you

Tell me something you can do to be understood.

Thank you

Decide to be in your life fully and tell me what you notice.

Thank you
Decide to not be in your life fully and tell me what you notice.
Thank you

Body Awareness
Put your attention on your body and tell me what you notice.
Thank you

Tell me everything about a physical challenge you are having and how it feels in your body.
Thank you
If this physical challenge could speak, tell me what it would say.
Thank you

Co-Dependency
Tell me a way you have depended on others for your happiness.
Thank you
Tell me another way you can find happiness.
Thank you

Tell me how you have depended on others to complete you.
Thank you
Tell me a decision you could make.
Thank you

Tell me how you have given yourself up in relationships with others.
Thank you
Tell me a decision you could make.
Thank you

Tell me what you do to get others to like you.
Thank you
Tell me a decision you could make.

Thank you

Tell me about you not trusting your own feelings.
Thank you
Tell me what you can do to trust your own feelings.
Thank you

Tell me how you have compared yourself to others.
Thank you
Tell me a decision you could make.
Thank you

Boundaries
Tell me a way you would like others to relate to you.
Thank you
Tell me a way you would like to relate to others.
Thank you

Communication
Tell me some concerns you have about listening honestly to others.
Thank you
Tell me some concerns you have about speaking honestly to others.
Thank you
Tell me a way you deny telling the truth to yourself and others.
Thank you
Tell me what you find difficult to face.
Thank you
Tell me how you can develop the ability to tell the truth to yourself and others.
Thank you

Personal Power
Tell me a way you give over your personal power to others.
Thank you

Tell me what it is that you are reluctant to face in yourself and present to others.
Thank you

Rejection
Tell me a way you have felt rejected or criticized by another.
Thank you
Tell me a way you have rejected or criticized others.
Thank you

Tell me a way you have felt rejected or criticized by another.
Thank you
Tell me how you have rejected or criticized yourself.
Thank you
Tell me what you can do to handle your feelings of rejection or criticalness in the future.
Thank you

Intimacy
Tell me something that you have done in a relationship that helped you get closer to another.
Thank you
Tell me something that you have done in a relationship that was not helpful in getting closer to another.
Thank you

Imagine yourself getting close to another and tell me what you experience.
Thank you
Tell me a decision you can make to get closer to others.
Thank you

Help
Tell me how you can help your partner in your relationship get closer to you.
Thank you
Tell me how your partner can help you.
Thank you

Couples
Tell me something you like about me.
Thank you.
Tell me something you think we agree on.
Thank you.
Tell me something about yourself you think I should know.
Thank you

Tell me an error you have made in our relationship.
Thank you
Tell me what you have learned from this.
Thank you
Tell me something you would do differently in a similar situation in the future.
Thank you
Tell me something you are grateful for in our relationship.
Thank you
Tell me something you want to thank me for.
Thank you

Responsibility
Tell me something you blame another for.
Thank you
Tell me something that person is responsible for.
Thank you
Tell me what you are responsible for.
Thank you

Personality

Be in the personality of _____ and tell me about yourself.

Thank you

Tell me what you are trying to do by being in the personality of _____.

Thank you

Tell me a decision you could make.

Thank you

(Examples of Personalities: Controller, Self-Critic, Procrastinator, Protector, Victim, Saboteur, Hero, Lost Child, Caretaker, Scapegoat, Mascot, Hippie, Late arriver, Saint, Saviour, Rebel, Vixen, Goddess, Enabler, Rescuer, Clown, Perfectionist, etc.)

Self-Empowerment

Be in the personality of _____ and tell me what you notice.

Thank you

Feel really good about being _____ and tell me what you experience.

(Examples: The Creator, Leader, Teacher, Adventurer, Pioneer, Asserter, Decider, Prosperous one, Peacemaker, Healer, Communicator, Risk-taker, etc)

Money

Tell me what money is.

Thank you.

Tell me what money is not.

Thank you.

Give me an example that money is good.

Thank you.

Give me an example that money is bad.

Thank you.
Tell me any comments you have.
Thank you.

Tell me how you want to earn money in a way that uplifts yourself and others.
Thank you.
Tell me how you want to spend money in a way that uplifts yourself and others.
Thank you.

Compulsions/Addictions
Tell me a behaviour of yours that is compulsive or addictive in your own estimation.
Thank you.
Tell me in detail what you normally do when you act on this behaviour.
Thank you.

Tell me a behaviour of yours that is compulsive or addictive in your own estimation.
Thank you
Get the idea of having the urge to act on this behaviour and not acting on it and tell me what you experience.
Thank you
Tell me what you can do to get support to face this experience.
Thank you

CHAPTER 16

CO-EVOLUTION INSIGHT AND AUTHENTICITY GROUPS

So far we have applied the dynamics of Co-evolution to one-on-one relating or dyads but the dynamics can also be used to accelerate the development of awareness in a group setting.

RESONANCE

An interesting phenomenon called resonance is accentuated more in a group compared to one-on-one relating. Resonance happens in music when one note is plucked on a stringed instrument causing the same note on another instrument to vibrate in sympathy without being plucked. In a similar way, when authenticity is increased and group members are communicating their insights, there is a tendency for others in the group to contact similar truths within themselves. There is a sense of group consciousness that develops where all members as a team are co-operatively engaged in digging into a great mystery and sharing their realizations with one another for the benefit of all. It's a democratic process, refreshingly different from the hierarchal dispensation of truth that is characteristic of traditional religions.

Everyone is an equal player yet adds a unique individual perspective that contributes to the collective upliftment of each person in the group. As people communicate and are fully understood without interruption, communication cycles are completed and "aha" experiences and epiphanies become commonplace. People leave the group with greater consciousness of Self, life and others, instead of simply contemplating on their own. In order to allow the fullest participation of all members of the group, these groups are kept to only 3-6 members.

There are two types of Co-evolution groups: an Insight group and an Authenticity Group.

THE CO-EVOLUTION INSIGHT GROUP

The procedure of the Insight group is almost the opposite of the dyad process yet the end result is the same. In a dyad we start off with a question such as "Who am I?" and end up with a first-hand insight or direct experience that originates from ourselves. In an Insight group we select an answer that has originated from someone else's questioning and contemplate it to determine the validity of it. We do not take this answer as the gospel truth. We understand that it is dogma but do not accept or reject it. As we contemplate the answer, we vicariously stimulate our first-hand insights that may or may not be related to the original. Each person's sharing becomes the catalyst for others' emerging insights. Here is how the group works:

PROCEDURE FOR THE INSIGHT GROUP

1. In a private room, individuals sit in chairs in a circle in groups of 3 to 5 people. They sit a comfortable distance apart so they can easily hear each other speaking. Each group of

3-5 should be a sufficient distance apart so that it lessens the distraction of members hearing others in other circles. They agree to share in the group for a set period of time (30, 40, 50 or 60 minutes).

2. The group decides on a concept to contemplate. A designated monitor (who also has the role of timer) writes it on a piece of paper and places it in the centre of each circle. E.g. "an individual is a non-physical being, divine in nature".

3. The monitor (who can be part of a group or as an outside facilitator) says: "Begin contemplating".

4. Each individual with eyes open or closed goes into silence and begins contemplating the concept. Each person is to regard the concept as an assumption and not an absolute truth until, in his/her own experience, he/she has come to an insight that corroborates it, expands it or proves it not to be true.

5. When an individual feels the urge or the inner pressure to share a thought, feeling or experience, he/she should pause to let the thought, feeling or experience develop into more clarity and then share it with the group. That which is shared can be related or not related to the concept being contemplated. It can be in agreement or disagreement with the concept.

6. The speaker should avoid using the term you as this could be construed as referring to another person in the group and runs the risk of being interpreted as an evaluation. Whenever possible, the speaker should use the term "I" if the communication is really about him/herself and "we" if the communication is more theoretical. Each person should only take no longer than 2-3 minutes to complete the communication, paying attention to give others an equal amount of time to share.

7. Group members should open their eyes and silently maintain eye contact with the person speaking without nodding,

getting into a discussion, offering agreement, disagreement or positive or negative evaluation of any kind. The listeners should avoid trying to facilitate the communication by asking for more details or encouraging the person to share more. Instead they should try to understand as well as they can and accept the extent of the sharing that is given.

8. When they have understood what has been shared, they are each simply to say "Thank you" to the one who communicated.

9. If members of the group say: "Thank you" before the speaker is finished, the speaker is to continue speaking until he/she has completed the thought.

10. If a member of the group does not completely understand what the speaker has communicated they can say:
    -   "Say that again" to have them repeat the communication;
    -   "Summarize that" if he/she has not understood the essence of what was said; or
    -   "Clarify _____ (insert the term that was not understood) if he/she did not understand a word or concept that was communicated.

11. When the communication has been completed by the speaker and understood by the listeners, all members in the group go back into silent communication and steps 4-10 are repeated when anyone else in the group chooses to share. The communication does not need to occur in any order. Anyone can communicate when they feel the inner necessity to do so.

12. As more communication occurs in the circle, speakers should avoid referring to anything others have said, or direct their communication specifically at another as well as refraining from giving advice.

13. Five minutes before the end of the allotted time of the group, the monitor is to say "five more minutes" and then

at two minutes remaining "two more minutes" and then "Complete your thought and thank the speaker", when the time period is up.

IMPORTANT DISTINCTIONS

It is important to distinguish this group from a discussion group. In a discussion group there is often a presentation of study material and a period of sharing where people present their ideas in a fairly linear manner as one person adds their ideas to others and agrees or disagrees as the discussion progresses. There is often a lot of interruption and communication and understanding is often incomplete. People can get their backs up defending their positions and others can monopolize the discussion. The interchange often stays on a superficial, intellectual level and insights are not very deep. In a Co-evolution Insight group, there is no discussion and the relating is not linear. We spontaneously share without any relation to what the previous person said. Because there is no disagreement or agreement, we feel free to share whatever is really coming up sans judgment. Communication gets completed and, as a result, profound insights can occur. Even though it is not a discussion group, the Insight group can be a great addition to a discussion group and a wonderful way to help individuals develop deeper insights about any spiritual literature.

Here are some steps to include this Co-evolution process in any discussion group:

o   a welcoming and introduction to the process
o   a brief relaxation exercise
o   a short reading of spiritual or philosophical literature
o   a 10- to 15-minute discussion of the central idea in the literature
o   a selection of a central concept for contemplation

o   participation in the co-evolution insight group
o   a brief sharing of each person's important insights at the end
    of the time limit and then goodbyes

THE CO-EVOLUTION
AUTHENTICITY GROUP

The Authenticity Group is similar to the Insight group except
there is no central concept that everyone is contemplating. In the
Authenticity Group, the subject is Self. You all sit and notice what
your present-time real experiences of yourselves are. Some people
may find it useful to use a question such as: "What is the truth about
me right now?" or "What am I experiencing in my life?" or "How
am I really feeling in this present moment?" You endeavour to get in
touch with what is going on inside without denying, minimalizing,
suppressing or dramatizing it and then communicate it to the group.
You allow yourselves to be authentic, i.e. try to have your external
self-presentation match your inner experience. "I am feeling really
shitty right now. My life sucks". Or "I am just in a new relationship
and I am really nervous". Or "There is a deep inner peace that I am
getting in touch with. It feels warm and inviting".

In the safe and non-judgmental atmosphere, you can allow
yourselves to be nakedly honest. The sharing can be intimately
human and profound. You can communicate your deepest fears,
anger and sadness and most expansive elation. You can let your
emotions out. Because there are more people to relate to, the contact
and acknowledgement with others is greater. You can trust, risk
and let go more easily. And often what happens in this group is a
common theme appears as if by magic to which everyone connects
strongly. You resonate with each other as your unique viewpoints
of this common experience is shared and instead of feeling alone in
this Co-evolutionary universe you will feel connected in this thing

called life, struggling together with it and innocently trying to figure out its mystery.

> *"It is by going down into the abyss that we recover the treasures of life. Where you stumble, there lies your treasure. The very cave you were afraid to enter turns out to be the source of what you were looking for. The damned thing in the cave that was so dreaded has become the center."*
>
> /
> —Joseph Campbell

COMMON INITIAL CONCERNS ABOUT THE CO-EVOLUTION GROUP AND HOW TO HANDLE THEM.

These are some common concerns that first-time participants have. It is beneficial to mention these before engaging in the group. It is often good after the group is finished to ask for comments on the process. Frequently these issues will be mentioned and the best way to address them is by using the responses below.

Reluctance to communicate

Initially, most first-time members find it difficult to communicate. Sometimes this is due to social shyness or the fact that there is a higher level of contact that they are experiencing with others compared to normal life. It should be explained that this increased attention is a benefit, that other members' attention on a specific topic, when added to his/her own attention, augments the energy that each person has to inquire within, making breakthroughs in awareness much more possible. With this higher level of contact, the person may feel caught between the social shyness and a deeper internal pressure to share and break through this introversion. A solution is to suggest to new members that they notice this shyness and just take the risk to communicate anyways by saying something like: "I feel shy about talking". Telling the truth about this reduces the pressure he/she may feel inside and, in many cases, they can experience an important social breakthrough. Once this initial communication is made and the person experiences that he/she is received without judgment, it becomes easier to be a part of the group.

Lack of feedback

Sometimes first-time participants in a Co-Evolution group will voice that they are uncomfortable with not being able to nod their head or say "yes" or give any other ongoing body language or verbal acknowledgement while the person is speaking.

It should be explained that the purpose of refraining from these usual conversational methods is to allow the speaker to fully communicate his/her truth without any positive or negative input from the listeners. Nodding or saying "yes" or any other form of approval can subtly influence a speaker to speak more about what the listener is nodding to and avoid speaking about what is really true for the speaker. It should be explained that socially we are so programmed to seek acceptance from others and avoid the reality of our own experience that we do this unconsciously given the subtle approval or disapproval signals from others. Participants should be told that this discomfort will be temporary and be replaced with an appreciation of how important this guideline is when they have the experience of being able to freely communicate without worrying about what others think.

Silence

Sometimes first-time members will find the silence uncomfortable in the group while all members contemplate. It should be explained that this is a natural experience for first-time participants, as this does not occur in normal conversation. In normal conversation, people are constantly interrupted and people are expected to come up with instant responses in a continual back and forth repartee. As a result, much of our relating is superficial and false, as people don't often speak the truth. It should be explained that the quality of sharing in the group is not common in normal conversation and that this guideline has a specific reason: we need time to look inside to contact what is real and this requires time and silence. It is a great gift that we give others and ourselves when we do this. A suggestion could be given if this discomfort arises: to communicate to the group "I find it difficult to be silent". This is, in fact, what is arising as a true experience for the person. Oftentimes just this simple communication relieves the initial tension and the person then becomes more comfortable with the silence.

Not Commenting on Another's Sharing

Some participants may find it difficult to not comment on another's communication, especially when it relates to them. It should be explained that commenting on another's sharing could run the risk of adding in an evaluation or being interpreted as an evaluation by the speaker. If this happens it can seriously affect the future sharing of a participant if he/she feels the sharing will be evaluated. It is much better to just avoid commenting than have this situation occur.

Avoiding Advice

Sometimes people feel compelled to give advice when others present a problem. As the group's purpose is not set up to solve problems and there is no agreement for this, this is to be avoided. Giving advice can also be interpreted as a subtle evaluation and in fact many people would prefer to solve the problem themselves. If a participant wants to give advice to another, he/she should set aside the urge until after the session and then ask the person if he/she wants advice and give it only by permission.

Wanting to Answer Another's Question

Sometimes a person will share that they have a question or something he/she is confused about. For example, a person may say "I don't know what a relationship really is". Members of the group should consider this as any other sharing and acknowledge it with a "thank you" and avoid the temptation to give the person an answer. Participants should be allowed the dignity of struggling to find the answer for themselves as often the answer they receive from their own contemplation is much more appropriate to their life than the answer another can give. In addition, the act of finding the answer will develop the ability in that person to inquire much more deeply so that in the future they will have a greater ability to self-inspect.

The exception to this is if the person's question stimulates the same confusion in another participant. If this is so, the participant, in their own sharing, can share his/her own confusion as well as any insight they come up with in an attempt to answer the same question for his/herself. However, if one has an answer to another's question and wants to help by giving the answer, this should be avoided.

In some way, this situation is similar to wanting to give advice to another who has a problem. In this case, the person's problem is that he/she is in confusion and has a question. Giving an answer can have the same effect as giving advice.

The overall answer to all the above concerns is that a Co-Evolution Insight or Authenticity group uses a different way of relating than normal conversation. The guidelines in the Co-Evolution group have a specific purpose that is different than normal conversation: to improve the quality of the relating so that deep insight can occur. Typical every day conversation, even the kind of conversation that is experienced in discussion groups, cannot deliver these breakthroughs in such a short period of time.

It is worth dealing with the initial discomfort of the guidelines so that one can experience these insights. Once one has experienced the benefits of these new understandings, the rationale behind the guidelines will be appreciated.

The Co-evolution and Authenticity groups can be a wonderful addition to a psychotherapy or meditation weekend or an afternoon of dyads. As people communicate and as mutual understanding is established each time a communication cycle is completed, participants let go of layers of confusion, misunderstanding and withheld pain. Relief and healing happen. Hearts open to one another. The True Self shows up out of the mire of the mind and finds a new stability based on the insights of truth that each person accesses. As people collectively delve inward, the invisible cohesiveness that is inherent in life becomes self-evident and people leave the group feeling less alone and more willing to engage in the grand scheme of awakening in their lives.

> *"The separateness seen in the world is secondary. Beyond that world of opposites is an unseen but experienced unity and identity in us all."*
>
> —Joseph Campbell

CHAPTER 17

MIND AND EMOTIONAL CLEARING
(AKA ASSISTED SELF-INQUIRY)

Imagine the potential, if instead of two people doing 5-minute changeovers in the dyad format, one person received a series of selected instructions from a listening partner and then contemplated and then communicated for 1 to 1½ hours. How would it be if one person received that kind of concentrated help from someone while maintaining the listening skills of non-evaluation, non-influence, and full attention without offering advice? Would it be possible over a number of these sessions for people to resolve inner conflicts, dissolve limiting attitudes, let go of trauma and have crucial insights that could significantly help people in their lives?

Darn right!

The process would obviously require skillful training in order for the listening partner to facilitate. Even though it is not something that someone without training could do, I thought to mention it because, as I have clearly stated in this book, mind and emotional healing is an essential part of the spiritual path. Such a system has already been developed on the basis of Co-evolution. It is a very powerful process called Mind and Emotional Clearing (aka Assisted Self-Inquiry).

Charles Berner also developed this process in the 1950's and 1960's at his Institute of Ability in California. It came out of his research and testing of many therapeutic methods that were being developed by others at the time and out of his own enlightenment experiences of the nature of Self, life and others. Since that time, one of his main students, Lawrence Noyes of the Clearing Academy in Florida, continued experimenting and adding new techniques to the process. I have been a practitioner for over 25 years and I also continue contributing my own new techniques to the process.

HOW DOES CLEARING (OR ASSISTED SELF-INQUIRY WORK)?

Clearing is a structured process in which a Practitioner gives specific instructions suited to the issues a client is dealing with and ensures that the communication cycle (described in the dyad format) is continually completed and the client is consistently understood. The process is based on the understanding that problems are the result of:

- Overwhelming incidents that you were not able to fully experience
- Withheld communications to others associated with these experiences
- Erroneous beliefs and identifications connected to these incompletions
- False solutions or unrealistic decisions that don't work

As incomplete communications that were based in past experiences and misunderstandings in relationships are completed, deep-seated or unconscious barriers to a person's full engagement in life are dissolved. With a skilled practitioner, the process can free you from re-occurring negative patterns, beliefs, behaviours and improve your ability to get clear on your goals in life, accomplish them and enhance your relationships and fulfillment in life.

There is no psychoanalyzing; counseling with advice or subtle manipulation for you to look at your issues the way the therapist sees you. Clients come up with their own insights and emotional discharges that are much more life-changing than the "diagnosis" of an authority. It is also unlike traditional psychotherapy that views you and your mind as a composite personality that has been genetically programmed and shaped from developmental experiences over your lifetime.

It is based on a fundamentally more liberating set of assumptions:

- You are not your mind, but you have a mind and personality just like you have a body.
- You are the "true source" or the creator of your mind.
- You are a unique individual, divine in nature, already complete.
- You do not need to be improved; only your understanding of Self, Life and others and your ability to relate needs to be developed.

In a matter of 5-10 sessions, compared to months or years of other types of therapy, Clearing or Assisted Self-Inquiry can help you:

- Connect to the origin of your issues
- Complete your past relationships
- Dissolve inner tension, trauma and conflict
- Find peace in the real truth about the past
- Be free of the negative beliefs and false solutions that are holding you back

- Recover your ability to freely relate to others from your true being

Ultimately it helps you improve your ability to overcome the difficulties you are facing and take responsibility for how you have dysfunctionally created your life and sets you on a new path of creating a brighter future. As your mind is cleared, the heart opens, wisdom spontaneously occurs and the full magnificence of your true being shows up. To witness people in this modality suddenly become free of their mind and emerge in the magnificence of their True Self is one of the most satisfying experiences in my life.

CONCLUSION

We've come to a conclusion but it's not conclusive. Does the Co-evolution process really work? I've realized it does. I am 100% certain that it does. But you will have to decide for yourself. How? By trying out this process. Get a buddy and try out a dyad for 40 minutes taking 5-minute turns speaking and listening. Gather a few spiritual folks and do a Truth or Authenticity group. If you have some problems, get some Clearing sessions. Better yet, take an Enlightenment Intensive. Your conclusion is not very far away.

How will you know?

When you get there.

You'll know you're there when you get there. You will recognize your awakening when you awaken. That's the only way. And that's part of the problem on the spiritual path. You never know how close you are to an insight or awakening until it happens. Unfortunately, many of us give up just before the breakthrough. We get 95% of the way there and then decide to go back when all we needed to do was take one more step. The light switch is just around the corner and we stop searching and decide to stay in the dark.

So don't stay stuck. Don't settle for reading books about enlightenment and settling for intellectual ideas that seem to fit. Don't settle for getting temporary relief, getting calm or finding transitory bliss . . . all that fluffy new-age stuff. Don't settle for anything less. Less is well . . . just less. Actually it's less than less. It's nothing. You are either awake or you are not. Go for resolution. Go for transformation. Go for enlightenment. Go for the Truth. Rent a guru for a little while if you need to but don't let his dogma drive your karma. Become your own authority! Be your true source!

We folks out here in the u-n-I-verse need you. We need your unique point of view, presence, story, experience, love, understanding, all of it . . . all of you. I mean it . . . YOU. Who knows . . . your experience of the truth may be the next big new understanding we all need. You could be the next garage mechanic that becomes a Buddha. And the wonderful thing is, through Co-evolution, you don't have to be the Lone Ranger anymore. Call it what you like: Co-evolution, Democratic Spirituality, Partner-Assisted Inquiry, Dyadic Dialoging . . . whatever. Don't get stuck in the label. The main thing is this: try out this stuff. Be your own guru. Come to your own conclusions . . . try out this thing of you evolving me and me evolving you. No more dogma . . . just you doing it by yourself but together with the rest of us.

WOW!

RESOURCES

There have been a few books written on or reference the Enlightenment Intensive. These are some good ones that I recommend:

The Enlightenment Intensive: Dyad Communication as a Tool for Self-Realization
by Lawrence Noyes.1998, Frog, Ltd, a Division of North Atlantic Books

Tell Me Who You Are, By Jake Chapman, contact: Jake and Eva Chapman, The Old Manor House, The Green, Hanslope, MKI9 7LS (free download at: http://www.enlightenment-intensives.org.uk/TellMeWhoYouAre%28part1%29.pdf)

The Quantum Gods: The Origin and Nature of Matter and Consciousness, By Jeff Love available from iUniverse.com, Barnes and Noble, Amazon.com (contains info on the Enlightenment Intensive)

SOME FREE STUFF

Go to my website www.truesourceseminars.com
"Living from the Inside Out": a 25-page report on the 5 paths of awakened living.
"Common Pitfalls on the Spiritual Path and How to Avoid Them"

Lots of free articles i.e.

Why I don't Recommend a Sub-Arachnoid Hemorrhage to Get Enlightened"
"How to Get a License to be Yourself"
"The Wisdom of the Gasping Man"

Ask for a **free download of a 5-minute gong timer** CD so that you can start doing dyads with your circle of friends.

CLEARING (OR ASSISTED SELF-INQUIRY)

To find a Practitioner in your area go to:
www.truesourceseminars.com or e-mail: info@truesourceseminars.com
www.lawrencenoyes.com or e-mail: Lawrencenoyes@aol.com
The process can be done in-person or anywhere in the world by Skype. Many practitioners will offer you a complimentary exploratory session to help you get clear on what you want to achieve in your life, what is in the way and if the process can help you. **I offer 5 complimentary sessions per month. If you would like receive one contact me at my website below.** These may or may not be available depending on my travel schedule.

If you are interested in training to become a Clearing Practitioner, contact me through my website at: www.truesourceseminars.com

Enlightenment intensives around the world
For facilitators of the Enlightenment Intensive in your area, Google: "Enlightenment Intensive."

There are many people that give Enlightenment Intensives around the world. Sometimes they give the retreat under different names: Illumination Intensive, True Awakening, True Heart/True Mind, etc. Some give a traditional intensive according to the original version originated by Charles Berner and some have altered it. If you are interested in doing one of my retreats or one facilitated by people who have studied with me or one with a facilitator I recommend, contact me at: www.truesourceseminars.com

If you are interested in participating in an Enlightenment Intensive use the certificate at the end of this book to apply for a scholarship. A limited number of scholarships are available on each retreat.

GRATITUDE LIST

There are a number of people to whom I want to express my gratitude. They have all in many ways contributed to the life of this book:

My wonderful partner Heather Embree for her editing and her unrelenting loving emotional support to get this book done; Sandy Fiegehen for her editing and incredible support of me personally and professionally; Darlene Nicholson, Lise Gillis, Beth Clark, Victor Levytsky, Reinier de Smit and Brenda McMorrow who have provided such wonderful support as on-going staff and friends on my retreats; My three children Jesse, Jonathan and Leela who have kept me honest and authentic; My previous wife Linda who was my companion through thick and thin as we explored this path of co-evolution for 26 years; Lawrence Noyes for being such a strong, wise presence as a teacher and mentor in my life; Charles and Ava Berner for originating and developing this incredible work; Jeff Love for his writing, from which I borrowed, on the Enlightenment Intensive; Monica Piercy for intuiting that I was pregnant and about to give birth to this book; Doug Tyler who supported me to give my first E.I.; Anjali Hill and Thomas Koven my deep friends at the beginning of exploring this path; my mother Irene Scott for her indomitable spirit; my father Marvin Scott who taught me to be impeccable; my brothers Glenn, Jerry and Gordon for opening up my "Clown Chakra"; my cousin Laverne for being there when I needed him; Ralph my late dog who showed me how to "just be what you are"; and all the truth seekers and truth guides that have walked the spiritual path and cast aside dogma to find the guru in themselves. Without your love and presence, I would not exist.

WHO IS RUSSELL ALLEN SCOTT?

Russell is one of the new generations of no-dogma spiritual teachers. As the former owner of the Ecology Retreat Centre near Orangeville, Ontario, Canada, he pioneered programs in sustainable living and green building and received a broad experience in the many spiritual paths that he encountered there. For over 35 years through his one-to-one sessions and group retreats, he has been helping people awaken to their deeper meaning and purpose so they can walk in the beauty and honestly of who they really are with a clear mind and pure heart. He is also the author of *"Awakening the Guru in You—the Co-evolution Process"* and an accomplished singer/songwriter who sometimes pretends he is a Western Swami that sings Country and Eastern songs.

RUSSELL'S SELF DESCRIPTION

I am just me.

I am not this well-seasoned body, my neurotic personal history or my awkward ego; although there are many times I really quite enjoy playing in my personality. Much to the chagrin of some religious folks, I do exist (I must exist in order to contemplate my existence, right?). Yet I also do not exist because no one thing defines me, not even the concept of existence. Now what I am or my divine qualities are quite another story: pure consciousness, bliss, universal love, infinite potential, cosmic intelligence, unlimited energy, non-dual awareness, everything, nothing and all things in between and more. You can find these attributes accentuated more or less in whatever spiritual book you study. Better yet you'll find these qualities in the book of yourself.

I am really the same as you; I am just presenting myself uniquely and differently than you.

If I were to summarize it all I'd say this:

I am you

You are me

The guru is us.

Scholarship Certificate

You're invited to attend the next

Enlightenment Intensive

Discover the magnificence of your True Self at the next 4 1/2 day Enlightenment Intensive for the basic fee of meals/lodging plus staffing costs. (Approx $495.00 depending on location). The regular fee of the retreat is $1,500.00. At the end of the retreat, you are welcome to leave an additional donation for the retreat facilitator. Scholarships are limited to 10 people per retreat and are available on a first-come-first-serve basis.

To apply e-mail:

info@truesourceseminars.com
www.TrueSourceSeminars.com

TRUE S URCE

Seminars · Retreats · Counselling